Fair Rosamond, or, The Days of King Henry II: An Historical Romance

FAIR ROSAMOND;

OR

THE DAYS OF KING HENRY II.

AN HISTORICAL ROMANCE;

BY THOMAS MILLER,

AUTHOR OF "ROYSTON GOWER," "BEAUTIES OF THE COUNTRY,"
"A DAY IN THE WOODS," ETC.

Let us sit on the ground,
And tell sad stories.
King Richard II.

IN THREE VOLUMES.

VOL. II.

LONDON:
HENRY COLBURN, PUBLISHER,
GREAT MARLBOROUGH STREET.

1839.

LONDON :
PRINTED BY STEWART AND MURRAY,
OLD BAILEY.

FAIR ROSAMOND.

CHAPTER I.

Conscience and grace, to the profoundest pit!
I dare damnation : to this point I stand,—
That both the worlds I give to negligence,
Let come what comes ; only I'll be revenged.
SHAKSPEAR.

KING HENRY had but just witnessed the departure of Becket, thrown the short Norman cloak around his shoulders, and was awaiting the entrance of a menial whom he had despatched to saddle his palfrey, in order that he might return to Woodstock; when Eleanor suddenly entered the apartment. The King, however, was unconscious of her presence, thinking, probably, that it was some attendant, but continued to amuse himself by writing on the stained casement with a diamond. Nor were his thoughts at all engrossed with the subject which he was almost unconsciously recording; but dwelling more upon the results which were expected to follow the interview between Becket and the King of Scotland, and in which the peace of the northern shires was at stake. He had, however, scrawled several of the panes with the initials H. R., which were tastefully interwoven together, before he became aware of the presence of Eleanor.

"Leave you the palace to-night, my Lord?" said the Queen, eyeing his cloak and hunting-cap; for he was already equipped for his journey.

"Such is my purpose," replied the King briefly, "unless some unforeseen business calls for my longer delay here."

"Is there then nothing remaining here that can longer afford your Grace pleasure?" enquired the Queen, her dark eye kindling as she spoke, as if to announce the gathering storm. "Nothing that can induce your stay but matters of business?"

" I left several of my guests behind at the palace of Woodstock," stammered forth the King with a bad grace; " and as some of them were but recently in arms against our person, it behoveth us to look narrowly to their actions for a short time."

" Have not recourse to such petty excuses;" exclaimed the high-spirited Queen, with a look of withering scorn, " they become not a king. Say rather that the company of Rosamond Clifford is the great charm which hath drawn you so much to the palace of Woodstock of late."

" She whom you have named, abideth not at the palace, fair Queen," said Henry; " nor would we accuse our royal person wrongfully, since the charge floweth so readily from your own immaculate lips. 'Tis pity that your purity should have travelled so far to be at last tainted after so long a pilgrimage by Henry of England."

" Is this then all the satisfaction I am to receive at your hands?" exclaimed the angry Queen, her countenance darkening with rage. " Must I then have taunts and reproaches added to my injuries ? But, King though you be, beware! Let but yonder smooth-faced harlot cross my path, and by my father's bones, I swear, I will mar her beauty, and rend her limb from limb ; aye, though you were to plunge your own dagger into my heart the next moment, I would do it!" While she spoke her fine features seemed to blaze with wrath, and her eyes flashed with a brightness that was terrible to look upon.

" Eleanor," exclaimed the King, the dark spot at last gathering upon his brow, while he paced the apartment with rapid strides, " I have shared my throne with you, and raised you to the same dignity which I myself enjoy. Answer me ; have I ever charged you with those deeds which have been rumoured against you, and which have many a time brought the colour to my cheek, when I have heard them whispered about, by those who deemed not that I was within hearing? Is it honest, then, that you should charge me with matters that you have no proof of; while I remain silent to all the floating rumours that are abroad? By the holy sepulchre! not a soldier of the cross touches these shores, but he brings some new lay which was made on your feats at Palestine."

The features of the Queen became colourless; her passion could find no utterance; and while her lips faded to the same dim ashy hue as her cheeks, she said, " You then have listened to these slanders, and still kept your hand from your dagger. Would that I were again in my own realms! an hundred swords would have leaped from their scabbards, had these things but been whispered in Poictou and Aquitaine."

" Flatter not yourself that they are unknown there," said Henry, his fiery temper having now full rein; " they are borne even to the Holy Land. Bertrand de Born has shaped them into rude songs; and the troubadours sing to the gay court of France, how Henry of England, became possessed of two fair provinces, when, after long trial, they were rejected by an infidel and a christian king. Nay, they add, that he keeps in his court the old agent; and that Oliphant Ugglethred is at any time ready to come to terms with a new bidder."

" And knew you not of these things until now?" said the Queen, stung to the heart at these remarks, which at once struck at her pride and her conscience. " Harry of England, I did once love thee above all those who sued for my hand. When the Earl of Blois, and Geoffry of Anjou sought me in marriage, I hearkened to thee alone. Oh! I could tear out my heart, and blush to death, to think how foolish I have been. But from this hour thou shalt learn what it is to arouse a woman's vengeance. I know thou lovest me no longer. But, may my pillow prove a nest of adders, if I do not revenge thy hatred; —if I do not tear down and scatter on the winds this painted blossom that has sprung up between me and thy affection!"

" It would better become thee," said the King, " to look to thine own fame, if indeed thou hast any left that is worth the watching; and not thus be playing at bo-peep in every nook and oriel that presents either a shadow or a curtain, with Oliphant Ugglethred. Nay, thou mayest flash thine eyes. By the true Lord! an' thou darest to put thy threats in force against aught that I set value upon, better for thee if thou hadst thrust thine hand into a nest of deadly vipers. Mark me!" added he, raising his arm and voice together, " thou mayest think I have slept of late; but remember, that many an eye looks out for a king; and if thou dost but touch her that thou hast dared to breathe thy threats against, I will have this Ugglethred, this spy, this panderer whom thou fearest, put to the torture in the midst of mine own nobles. Nay, I will convene a holiday, and every tiller of the earth,—every serf that wears the symbol of servitude—shall hear him confess all that he hath ever known against thee." Saying which, he left the apartment

just as Ugglethred entered; nor did Henry acknowledge the low genuflection which the
ruffian made, as he held open the door for him
to pass.

"Thou hast come at a fitting hour," said
Eleanor, her eyes still flashing with anger, and
her brow lowering and dark as a thunder cloud.
"The King needed but thy hateful presence to
confirm his suspicions; and like evil, it waited
at the door."

"Where it hath often waited," replied the
ruffian, without changing a feature : "and was
·then called gentle Oliphant.   But it seems
that my watching hath availed but little, since
our secrets are at last bruited."

"Villain, thou hast not been playing the
eaves-dropper upon me," said the Queen; "but
what matter?" added she, "since Henry has at
last breathed out his suspicions. Thou hast
heard all then that hath passed between us?"

"For that matter, the door stood ajar,"
answered Ugglethred; "and I know no law
for closing a man's ears.   Beside I have

gathered nothing that is new; nor should I have waited, had you not summoned me hither."

"But mightest thou not have withdrawn?" continued Eleanor; "or at least concealed thyself when the king passed out, after hearing those foul whispers, which to me sounded like the hissing of serpents. Enough, thou seest the love that Henry bears to thee."

"Truly it is not so great as he beareth towards the lady Rosamond," said the ruffian, fixing his eyes on Eleanor as he spoke, and viewing with savage delight the terrible emotions which the hated name awakened.

"Thou hast a right touch of the devil in thee," said the excited Queen, "with which my mounting spirit can now keep pace. My revenge hath at last found an huge appetite. I will, with my own hand, strike dead the hated rival thou hast named."

"It were pity to mar so fair a piece of workmanship," said Ugglethred; "for she hath

a face that might almost allure a saint out of
heaven : and had she not slipped by me so
hastily, I would have shared her beauty with
his kingship.   But we are both flying our
hawks in the dark, for the quarry hath
escaped, nor have I as yet discovered her
retreat."

"Were she hidden in the deepest cavern of
the earth," said Eleanor, "my hatred would
find out her hiding-place.   Do thou but watch
the king at a safe distance, and thou wilt not
fail to discover where she lurks ; then will I
come upon them like a thunderbolt that leaps
unawares from the sky, and gratify my deep
revenge, by driving my dagger through both
their hearts at a blow.   Even here," said
she, striding up to the window like a fury,
while her long dark hair, which had slipped
from its braid, fell in wild disorder down her
face—"even here he has dared to interweave
her odious name with his own, as if her hated
image was not enough before me in his absence.

So let the remembrance perish! and it shall go hard if I make not as free room for the air of heaven to pass through that space without let or hindrance which their bodies now occupy." As she spoke, she drove the hilt of her dagger through the casement, which Henry had scribbled over with the diamond, and the stained glass fell rattling on the floor. "Do thou but bring me into her presence," continued Eleanor, "and I will hold it the best service thou hast done me. I have sworn by all that is good and evil, that I will be revenged upon her; and were she to die by other hands than my own, I would glut my hatred on her ashes in the grave. Death and darkness!" continued she, pacing to and fro as if she was mad, while her hair fell around her, and every now and then she threw it back in her fury; "to be thus tormented by him whom I took to make my name more honourable! Oh! I cannot utter all that my heart feels. Would to God that I had staid with the spiritless hawk of France, whom I could hood at pleasure, or let loose upon some paltry barn-door fowl, or flight of sparrows; but this falcon of England," added she, pressing her hands before her face, " would plunge his beak into my heart, and lay bare all that is there hidden." Then springing forward wildly, as if unconscious of what she did, she seized the hand of Ugglethred, and exclaimed, " Swear that thou wilt aid me in revenging these injuries, and I will weigh thee down with gold; nay, thou shalt have what thou hast so long coveted. I will give up this body of mine to enrich the agreement."

The villain swore that he would peril his soul in her service, and was about to draw her face to his own, to seal the bargain on her lips, when, as if suddenly recollecting herself, she drew her head back, and said, " Not now. I will ratify my vow when my revenge is glutted, and seal it with the blood of Rosamond Clifford."

As she spoke, she let fall the hand of the ruffian, and a slight shiver ran through the frame of Ugglethred while he gazed upon her;

for, hardened as he was, he could not look upon the savage beauty of the Queen without emotion. Eleanor stood like some beautiful goddess, whose nature has undergone a change; as if her frame could scarce hold the fierce anger and cruelty with which it had so suddenly became possessed, but was about to assume a shape in which the impress of the sterner passions would become moulded, and the whole burst forth into a form more terrible. As if she had called upon the gods to fill her with "dire cruelty," and they had sent down the evil powers to fulfil her request; and the eye could trace the progress of their work, which was fast overpowering her; for she staggered forward, and would have fallen had she not been caught by Ugglethred. The ruffian raised his voice to call for help; but the sound brought back Eleanor to her former consciousness; and she said, "Let no one be summoned hither, one witness is enough to this weakness." She put up her hair in the braid, and added, " it is over now. Thou wilt forget what thou hast

seen, good Oliphant; and be true to my cause
as steel to the hand."

"I would stand by thee, were we on the brink
of hell together," answered the dark-browed
ruffian, "and hunt out the haunt of this pale-
cheeked beauty, were she hidden in the bowels of
the earth."

Eleanor took a handful of gold pieces from
the pouch which hung at her girdle, and placing
them in the palm of Ugglethred, said, "Fail
me not;" and left the apartment.

"Thou art a daring devil," said the ruffian
to himself, as he fixed his eye upon her until
she quitted the room, "and would enter into a
league with the evil-one himself, to slake the
huge thirst of thy revenge. But not so fast,
mistress of mine. I will try to see yonder fair
slip of womanhood again, and if she consenteth
to my terms, devil a nail of thine shall mar her
beauty. But there is that cursed minstrel in
the path," added he, musing; "and I fear that
neither a lock of hair, nor a cup of the grape
of Gascony, will be so ready a bait again.

Somewhere is this Rosamond concealed, within an arrow's flight or two of the palace, or Vidal would not so often be found walking in the neighbouring pleasance with Mistress Maud. Thou wilt need much caution, Oliphant Ugglethred," continued he, still following up the train of his thoughts, " and must move about this work noiseless as a shadow. Thou must look with narrow eyes, and glide about stealthily as a serpent; and, if need be, put on a better look than those who mean true friendship,—carrying the look of Heaven in the face, and the feelings of hell in thè heart,—as many a better man hath done ere this. A very fiend is this Queen; and those who cross her path must be guarded; and to save one which her eye has made a victim, is as dangerous as rending the prey from the jaws of a hungry wolf. Curse her," added he aloud, as he quitted the apartment, " I know she hates me more than she does Satan himself. But it is some comfort to know that she also fears me." So saying, he placed the gold in a slip of his gaberdine, and

sallied forth to discover the hiding-place of
Rosamond, and avail himself of the advantages
of the most favourable bidder.   But we must
leave him to follow the fate of the more important personages of our story.

CHAPTER II.

I thought he had resembled King Henry,
In courage, courtship, and proportion :
But all his mind is bent to holiness,
To number " Ave Marias," on his beads :
His champions are, the prophets and apostles ;
His weapons, holy saws of sacred writ ;
His study is his tilt-yard, and his loves
Are brazen images of canonized saints.
King Henry VI.

Nothing material occurs in our story, until some time after the return of Becket from Lincoln ; when he was almost immediately made Primate of England. Firm to his promise, and secure in the good services of the Chancellor, Henry disregarded the murmurs of the Norman nobles, and preferred his faithful servant to the See of Canterbury, not doubting for a moment, but that he would prove a willing instrument to his royal pleasure. The king had heard of the sudden change which Becket's character had undergone; and was not a little surprised that the gay courtier should all at once become the ascetic churchman; but he smiled to himself when he thought of the merry moments they should pass together alone, when the Archbishop would lay aside his holiness, and again become the boon companion; for he never once doubted but that this excessive sanctity was but assumed to blind the people. Business, or pleasure had, on the one hand, confined the King to the neighbourhood of Oxford and Woodstock, while on the other it had detained the newly-made Archbishop at his diocese; so that they had scarcely ever met since the change had taken place in Becket, of which rumour spoke so loudly. Henry had, however, at length invited the prelate to Woodstock, for his late carousals had lacked much of their former spirit since his absence, and it was on the day that the Archbishop had accepted the King's invitation, that we again resume our narrative.

Two pampered domesties were pacing indolently along the chief gallery or hall of the palace, or sometimes lolling listlessly on the massy oaken benches, which stood ready for the convenience of attendants or messengers in waiting, when after much scandal, and many hazardous guesses that would have cost them their heads, had their conversation reached the King, they at length fell into discourse on the marvellous change which the Archbishop was announced to have undergone. Nor did they fail to magnify the wonders which they had heard of,—a part so necessary to true gossiping, that it may be considered its greatest charm ; for the wonder awakened is a kind of stimulant to the narrator to " lay it on." Neither will it be doubted for a moment, that in an age like that, which we are attempting to bring before the reader, when miracles were believed in, and superstition universally prevailed to an extent scarcely to be believed, the reformation of Becket was assigned to some mighty power. Some attributed it to a divine unction suddenly

imparted to him during his consecration; but
the lower orders had called in the agency of an
angel of light; a tough combat with Sathanas,
and the routing of a whole legion of fiends, who
had attempted to carry him away. But without
venturing an opinion on his sudden conversion,
—a point on which our ablest historians dis-
agree, regarding its sincerity, or hypocrisy,—
we will take up the conversation between the
two menials, which had by this time become
warm.

"Then I say his wits are gone a wool-gather-
ing," replied the fat attendant, to his companion, who had been dwelling upon some
miraculous description of the Archbishop,—
"What! to taste of no ale, which is of itself
meat and drink, then I say your great Prelate is
mad, for refusing the good things which Heaven
has sent him? Think you that the miracle
which was performed at the marriage of Cana,
when the water was changed into wine,—which,
after all was mayhap good strong ale,—would
have been done, were it not intended that man

should enjoy such good things? No, marry, it would have been changed to fennel-water, green, filthy, and stagnant, such as you say this witless prelate only drinks, if the saints had required us poor mortals to swallow such poison. I say that he is mad as a March hare."

" But they say he does these things that he may have power over the evil one," said the other, with a knowing shake of the head : " and further, I can tell thee, Clement, that he eateth such black, unwholesome bread, that the very dogs turn up their noses at the remnant of it. He also wears a hair shirt to mortify his body, so rough, that it is like feeling of a ginger-grater; and that if once pulled off and thrown on the ground, there are inhabitants enough lurking within, to walk away with it as easily as a pedlar trudges off with his empty pack. Nor would he slaughter one of these beloved back-biters, for a knight's ransom ; for they are of a choice breed; and their ancestors fed many a day on the blessed St. Dunstan, their true colour being a dusty black, which they have doubt-

less caught through being smoked in the
saint's smithy."

"No doubt, then, he holdeth it a waste of
water to wash himself," said Clement. "But
what has he done with his cooks and cup-bearers,
his grooms and lacqueys, his pages, knights, and
squires? Assuredly he has no need of these;
as one might do to boil his fennel-water, and
bake his black bread."

"There thou art wrong," answered the other,
"for his table is spread daily for the blind and
the lame; never had the roguish beggars such
a merry time. They need but to drag their
lazy bodies into the green lanes about Canterbury, and out sallies a whole troop of the
Archbishop's retainers to invite them to the
feast. The knaves are leaving off their
mummery and fortune-telling, and learning
to patter their prayers. You should have
seen Walter with the Wide-wallet, Billy the
Bezzler, Clement the Club-footed, Izaak the
Immoveable, and a few others of Walter's
ragged crew, how they did skip and caper

before the scot-ale, for very joy that the Archbishop had washed all their feet with his own hands, and given each of them four silver pennies."

"Ah! ah! ah! I will wager thee my buck-handled whittle, to thy silver-rimmed drinking horn, that they are merry enough together to-day," said Giles, laughing; "and that they get to jumping over the benches and tables, ere they have drunk their third cup, and are more like two boys let loose from labour, than a king and archbishop."

"Thou wouldst lose thy bet," replied the other; "for I can tell thee that since St. Dunstan appeared to him, he is strangely altered, and goeth up and down the cloisters of St. Bennet, wringing his hands all day long, and weeping aloud for his sins. Nay, they say that in the night, strange voices are heard in his chamber, and that music has played over his head while he was asleep, and that the musicians and the speakers were invisible to all but himself."

"Truly it is strange," answered Clement: "and methinks, were I to see him play these grave antics, I should laugh outright, as I have done many a time at his merry jests, when I have filled his wine-cup, and seen the tears roll down King Henry's cheeks with sheer laughter, and heard him beg of the witty chancellor to keep silence unless he meant to kill him with his jokes and gibes. Marry, 'tis very strange that one who could laugh, hunt, joke, empty his wine-cup at every turn, make a lady sigh sooner than any baron in hall or bower, and splinter a lance with the boldest that ever buckled on armour, should become so suddenly changed. I can scarcely believe it, nor will I, until I have trusted my own eyes. I will watch him narrowly at the banquet to-day, and if I have not two or three right merry jests to retail to thee to-night, then shall I begin to think that he is not the real Thomas à Becket."

"Think what pleaseth thee best," answered the other, looking out from a shot-hole which inwardly widened to a kind of large niche.

" Yonder cometh the Archbishop, and thou wilt now be able to judge for thyself. By the true Lord! he seemeth but the shadow of his former self;—his cheeks are almost as transparent as a horn lanthern; but he is mounted on a brave steed; and, by the mass! never did priest before sit in a saddle like to him."

" I will in then," said Clement, " and like a dog give mouth that the hunter may know there is game a-foot." So saying, he entered a side-door to apprise Henry of Becket's approach.

Meantime the Archbishop had alighted, and as he proceeded with slow and measured steps across the court-yard which led to the inner entrance of the palace, a tall gaunt stag-hound reared itself up beside him in acknowledgment of their former acquaintanceship. Becket struck down the noble animal with indignity, as if he was ashamed of being recognized by an old favourite that had no respect for his sanctity, and only reminded him of other days, when he was the foremost in the chase, with his loud whoop and hallo. The old hound slunk away in seeming astonishment, and made a dead pause when he had retired a few paces, and, running his eyes once more over the form of the prelate, as if to assure himself that he was not mistaken, he uttered a deep internal growl, and stretched his huge length on the pavement.

Becket swept along through the vaulted gallery, to the upper room which Clement conducted him to, and however coarse his undergarments might be, his long dalmatica, which trailed along the floor, and rustled over the green rushes with which it was strown, was made of the costliest material, and richly ornamented with embroidery, while the bottom was trimmed with the choicest ermine, of more than a hand's breadth. His features had, however, undergone a great alteration; prayer and penance had left their traces upon his brow, and he seemed much older since the day that he set out in such pomp and grandeur, on his embassy to Lincoln. That which before had given such a pleasing expression to his fine

face, was now changed to a look of deep awe, a
kind of majestic seriousness, that seemed to sit
well enough upon the imposing figure of the
Archbishop, but had a strange appearance in
what was remembered of the gay chancellor.
Still the same fire lurked in his keen and pene-
trating eyes, and he carried his stately form as
erect as ever he had done in his gayest days;
and while he glanced around the arched gallery
through which he passed, his eye seemed to
kindle with the consciousness of what he was,
and every stride to announce that there moved
the proud Primate of England. Behind him
crept the grave monk Gryme, gliding along like
a shadow, with his head bent and his eyes
rivetted on the floor, while his long grey mantle
added to the appearance of his gravity: he
halted by the doorway which Becket entered.

The apartment which the Archbishop had
now gained, was that which had so often rung
with his own laughter, when he shared the carousals of the monarch; nor had he stood above
a moment or two, before king Henry sprang

from behind a pillar where he had concealed himself, and bounding forth unawares, placed his hands upon the shoulders of the Primate and leaped clean over his head. Henry laughed aloud when he had accomplished this feat, a trick which he had played off an hundred times before on Becket in former days, when they both were accustomed to amuse themselves by leaping over the settles and tables. Becket, however, moved not a muscle of his solemn countenance, but preserved his stern and iron composure, while the monarch gave vent to his own merriment in many a loud explosion of laughter. No sooner, however, did the good-hearted king's glance fall upon the solemn and unmoved features of the Archbishop, than his countenance instantly changed, and approaching him with a look of tenderness and anxiety, he said, " Ar't ill, my dear Becket?—speak what aileth thee ? shall we summon our Leech hither ?"

" Not ill, my liege," replied the proud churchman, who was somewhat chafed at the very familiar manner in which Henry had introduced

himself; for Becket had made himself up for
this interview, and intended striking the king
at once with an idea of awe for the sanctity of
his character; but such an unexpected recog-
nition in the old familiar manner of other times
had upset his dignity, and he was indeed vexed
to the heart.

"Not ill, my liege!" echoed Henry, whose
feelings were really then straight-forward, and
who was glad to see his old favourite, but felt
annoyed at the coldness with which his offered
kindness was received. "What the devil aileth
thee, then, that thou bringest such a cold
winter in thy looks? that thou comest with such
a funeral face to our banquet, and lookest upon
an old friend, as if thou wouldst freeze him to
death?"

Becket felt ashamed at this rebuke, and had
not his pride whispered him, that it would be
beneath the dignity of his holy calling, to unbend
his austere brow and receive the kind greeting of
the king, as he had done beforetime, he would
at once have embraced him; as it was, how-

ever, he took another course and thus spoke.
" Banquets and merry-makings, my liege, but
ill accord with the holy-office which Heaven has
called upon me to fulfil. I had thought that
your Grace needed some spiritual advice when
you summoned me hither, and came prepared to
offer you such, as a poor sinner might give,
whose days and nights have of late been spent
in penitence and prayer."

"Ah ! ah ! ah ! why thou playest thy part
like a very Archbishop," said Henry, laughing,
but not in that hearty manner which he was
accustomed to do when really merry: it was a
kind of laughter which belied itself, and was at
variance with the true feelings of the monarch
at that moment ; for the features of Becket were
still as serious, as if he was looking upon the
face of the dead, and Henry passed his hand
over his own brow as if to assure himself that he
was still awake. " Thou art but jesting with
me," continued he; " come, thou hast played the
saint long enough, now let a little of the sinner
out; this guarded conduct is well enough for

the world; but thou hast no need to play it off before ourselves."

" I play no part, my liege," replied Becket, in the same cold tone which he had from the first assumed; " I am what Heaven has made me, a changed man, wholly devoted to the service of God and the holy Church."

" And hast thou left no part to be devoted to my service?" said Henry, the dark shade gathering upon his brow. "Or hast thou entirely shut me out, who made thee what thou art? I do fear me that this sudden change forebodes no good to myself. Confess it, thou wouldst overleap our head, as we did thine, but now; oh! I fear I have been deceived in thee! Answer me; what have I done that I should deserve this coldness from thy hands?" The King averted his face when he had spoken, and attempted to hide the emotion under which he laboured.

" To me your Highness hath ever been kind," answered the Archbishop, his eyes rivetted upon the floor as if ashamed of looking Henry in the face; " and, saving the things which are of Heaven, will ever find me a faithful servant, and one ready to do your bidding to the utmost of my power. But,"—

" Enough, enough!" said Henry, pacing the apartment under great excitement, " I understand thee now; rumour hath for once rumoured aright. I will not hear thy buts and ifs. Oh, fool that I have been! I made thee Archbishop, that through thy hands I might lessen this overgrown power of the church. Thou hast deceived me; and would put in thy buts as men put up walls where land is parcelled out, until thou wouldst not even leave a footpath for a king to tread, unless it brought some benefit to the church."

" You do me wrong, my liege," said Becket, speaking in a bolder tone than he had hitherto done; " nor can you name an instance in which I have sought to infringe upon your royal liberty, or interfere with the privileges which belong to the throne; nor have I a wish but to further your renown; and, saving my duty to God, the

church, His Holiness the Pope, and my own
conscience, I am as willing to serve your Grace
as ever I have done, or did, ere I dedicated myself to Heaven."

"Disguise it as thou wilt," said Henry, in a
tone of voice which bespoke more sorrow than
anger, "thou art changed to me. Thou wert
not wont to call in these salvos. Pope, church,
and conscience, were forgotten when I needed
thy service; thou wert true to me, and I did
love thee." He buried his face in his hands
for a moment ere he could proceed; so much
did he feel this separation of friendship; it was
but for a moment, and he again assumed an
apparent composure while he thus proceeded:
"Becket, I did then love thee, ah, more than a
very brother. I preferred thee before any of my
high-born nobles. I made thee the companion
of all my pleasures. I imparted to thee all my
bosom secrets; leaving even my very honour
in thy hands. My heart harboured no feeling
that I kept from thee. My mind engendered
no thought that did not become thine own. I

made thee my second self. I studied to leave thee nothing to wish for. How art thou requiting me? By snowing down thy cold sanctity until it freezes upon my very heart: by spurning the ladder, up which thou hast climbed to this height of holiness. I fear me that I see as clearly into thy thoughts, as if they were graven on brass. Heaven grant that I read not aright!" So saying, and without waiting until the Archbishop replied, Henry left the apartment, for his feelings were fast outgrowing all command.

Once did Becket move, as if he meditated throwing himself at the King's feet, and vowing his service until death; but Henry had gone ere the resolution had put itself into action, and he stood gazing upon the blank and open doorway, as if he yet hesitated whether to follow him. " I have gone too far," were the first thoughts that rushed upon his mind when left alone; but I will heal this breach; for my heart hath still a yearning towards him. Alas! he has given me a power which places me beyond his reach. He has made me what he never can unmake again. I cannot serve him and Heaven, and be honest. I cannot serve God and man, and remain just to both. That which I have done I must undo; my duty is no longer what it was. He guesseth rightly; I am changed even to myself; I am not what I have been. The dignity of Heaven is in my keeping; —the church of Christ is entrusted to my care, and needeth a watchful shepherd."

While these thoughts were passing through his mind, he heard the voice of the King in the gallery exclaiming, " Assuredly thou liest, sir knight; he dare not do such a bold deed without my permission." An answer was made, but in so low a voice, that it reached not the ears of the Archbishop; and in another instant Henry re-entered the apartment, — his face flaming with rage. He was followed by a knight, whose bold cheek blanched the instant he encountered the fixed gaze of Becket. Henry also fixed his keen eyes upon the Prelate, and pointing to the knight, said, " Hast thou dared to excommunicate William de Eynesford, here present, without our permission?"

"Thy permission!" exclaimed Becket, taking fire in an instant, and turning upon the King with a look of angry pride, and astonishment,—"Whenever didst thou hear that the Primate of England had to stoop for permission to punish any rebellious son, who had disobeyed the holy mandates of the Church?"

"Is he not a military tenant of the Crown?" said Henry, his countenance flushed with rage, and his eyes gleaming on Becket with a fierce and steadfast glance. "Wert thou not aware long before the ill-starred hour I gave to thee the primacy, that no vassal who held *in capite* of the Crown, should be excommunicated without my sanction? Absolve him instantly."

"That will I not do," said Becket, in his turn bristling up, and looking indignantly upon the Monarch :—"It is not for you, my liege, to command whom I shall excommunicate, and whom absolve ; that power belongs to the

Church alone. Nor will I relinquish its holy rights."

It is almost impossible to describe the countenance of the King at that moment; speechless with passion, he stood with quivering lips, and eyes that seemed to flash forth fire: twice did his hand clutch the hilt of the dagger in his belt, and was again withdrawn; when, just as he was about to give vent to his rage, Gryme, who had been a witness of the whole scene from the outer passage, entered the apartment. It was not the presence of the monk that prevented the monarch from giving explosion to his wrath, but the sound of footsteps caused him suddenly to turn his head, and he at once became conscious that he was lowering his dignity, by thus exposing himself before De Eynesford and Gryme, and the thought called up all his pride; and in a moment he felt that Becket was obtaining a triumph over him, by showing that he had power to move him to such an extent. Turning, therefore, suddenly round, and frowning upon the Archbishop as he passed, he bade the knight to follow, and left the apartment.

"Follow his Grace," said Gryme, ere the footsteps of the King had ceased to sound in the vaulted passage; "lose no time, holy father, in absolving this knight from his sentence, lest his highness should come to some sudden resolve, for he parted with danger in his eye; and you well know——"

"Hold thy peace," replied the Primate, speaking sharply: "thinkest thou that I am to be frightened into obedience by threats and angry looks, like a menial who bows at the board of his master. No, by my holy order, I would excommunicate the king himself, if he dared to eject a priest, like this proud knight De Eynesford, from the church in which I had placed him."

" But this sudden breach," continued Gryme, who knew enough of King Henry's character to feel satisfied that where he once took a dislike, he rarely forgave the offender:—" may it not lead to difficulties, nay, even danger? Bethink you, holy father, it were better to absolve the knight at once, and ——"

"Open a pathway for a thousand abuses," said the Archbishop, interrupting him : " I tell thee it must not be. If I but once yield to these inroads, the Church might as well be without a head. No, I will be the Primate of England, or nothing. I am no dog to keep my watch beside the gates, to bark when I am bidden, and keep silence when a finger is uplifted; I will keep honest guard over the Church, let what may befall me."

" I speak but out of love for yourself, reverend father," proceeded Gryme in a more subdued tone; "this quarrel with the King will be a triumph to your enemies,—it will be accomplishing that against yourself, which they have so long attempted in vain to achieve."

" It matters not," replied the Prelate, heaving a faint sigh; "it is the will of Heaven that I should pursue this course; my path is still onward, if even I perish, Gryme," added he after a long pause, and with deep emotion. "I know thou meanest well; but I have foreseen this from the first; and if the King will no longer accept me as a friend, he shall find in me an honourable enemy:—the rights of the Church shall never be trampled under foot with impunity while I wield the pastoral crook over it. Let us begone; I will betake me to my sceptre; I will uplift the holy cross; and woe be to those who dare to wrench it from my grasp."

"Assuredly you will not go without taking a farewell of his Highness," said Gryme. "Bethink you of what may be the consequence of this abrupt departure——"

The speech of the monk was cut short by the entrance of an attendant, who with a smile of grim mockery, came to announce that the King would dispense with the presence of the Primate at his table, and that his steed stood ready accoutred without.

Becket bit his lip when he heard the message, and without deigning to reply, he stepped hurriedly along the passage; and throwing himself into the saddle with an agility that would have

done credit to any knight who was about to
rush into the combat, he set off at a very different rate to that at which he came ; and which,
although it would have seemed very befitting
for one about to join the chase, scarcely accorded with the dignity of the Archbishop of
Canterbury. Gryme followed soon after as he
best could, but not without being saluted by a
loud peal of laughter from the archers who
guarded the postern ; and he was soon lost in
the path that wound around an avenue of oaks,
the broad branches of which gave such a forest-
like look to the Park.

CHAPTER III.

Now I feel
Of what coarse metal thou art moulded—Envy.
How eagerly you follow my disgraces,
As if it fed ye ; and how sleek and wanton
Ye appear in everything may bring my ruin.
Follow your envious courses, men of malice !
                                        SHAKSPEAR.

IN the very hall where King Henry held his
feast after storming the castle, were assembled
several of the Norman nobles and bishops,
some of whom had been invited by the monarch
to share the welcome provided for Becket, and
others who had contrived by stratagem, favour,
and a hundred other old courtly tricks, to get
themselves admitted on the occasion. Although
unknown to the archbishop, great preparations
had been made by the monarch for the meeting
at Woodstock, and as such things were seldom

done, but on great occasions, the secret soon
flew abroad. As may be expected, the sudden
changing of Becket from the gay courtier, to
the ascetic churchman, was the common topic
of all England ; for it had turned out the very
reverse of what even the prelate's enemies had
calculated, as they expected nothing less than a
drunken, roystering, gay, and reckless Primate,
and in place thereof, found the most rigid
disciplinarian of fasts, prayer, and penances,
who had ever filled the holy see. However
the cry burst out as loudly then on the other
hand ; for where there is once a dislike, no
matter what course the object of it may take,
the party who have made up their hearts to con-
demn, are never long at a loss to find out some
new cause of complaint. So on this occasion,
the change was too sudden to become sincere ;
others contended that it was but taken up for a
blind ; while a few who carried matters to the
opposite extremity, hesitated not to attribute
it all to a miracle ; and many shook their
heads knowingly, and said, " Time will tell."

But it was amongst the Norman nobles and bishops, (for the latter were mostly of the same country,) where the greatest envy and hatred lurked, as no Saxon had been appointed to a station of such eminence, since the invasion of the Conqueror. Many there were who had assembled more out of curiosity than aught beside, wishing to see how the gay Chancellor would play the avowed Saint.

Amongst the chief of those thus congregated together, were the Archbishop of York, Hilary Bishop of Chichester, and Gilbert Foliot Bishop of Hereford, all of them enemies of Becket's. Yet, like true courtiers, determined to shape their course according to circumstances; a plan which some of the divines of the present day do not hesitate to adopt. Some were conversing together in a group; others walked apart, while one or two were holding earnest converse in the deep niches of the windows, all of course unconscious of what had taken place.

"I shall yet win my gage," said the Earl of Leicester, addressing a tall knight in armour:

"for we hear of no change: he still abandons his palfreys to patter his prayers, and herds with ghostly monks and friars, in place of sallying out at the head of his grooms, and giving the hollo to his hounds."

"Right loath shall I be to part with deep-throated Rud, and broad-chested Balder," replied the night; "for a brace of braver hounds never hung at the throat of a fallow-deer; but if we do not see him drink healths three-deep, and crack jokes with the merriest before moon-rise, thine own portcullis shall close upon them ere another day is down."

"E'en be it so," replied the Earl; "and if he still stick to the saint, thou shalt hear the hoofs of my bonny black steed beating across thy drawbridge before the tolling of to-morrow's curfew."

Turning to the bishops who stood conversing in the shadow of the oriel, thus ran the tenure of their discourse: "From whom didst thou gather these tidings?" said Hilary of Chichester, turning to Gilbert Foliot.

" From one who is better acquainted with the character of the queen, than either you or I," was the answer: "I tell thee that she hath long been studying how to revenge herself upon the king, for the visits he pays to the fair maid ycleped Rosamond, whom he somewhere harboureth like a hart in the thicket; it is a dainty piece of game."

" But may she not have ventured a notch too much upon the talley in her reckoning?" said the Bishop of Chichester; " bethink thee of the power Becket has obtained by the change. What benefit can she hope to reap through thus secretly abetting De Eynesford to eject the monk, any more than in setting her snares to work, to catch Becket in the affair of the castle of Rochester."

" Nay it is clear," replied Gilbert Foliot, " for by the clashing of flint and steel we produce fire; so in bringing together the king and primate is there hopes of raising a blaze; for both will burn without abating: thou well knowest that the primate, if once defied, is but as an ignited brand."

"Which blaze will extend even to the bishops,"
said Hilary of Chichester, "and they must be
content to stand a burning if they can but consume the building,—is it not so?"

"We strike down to rise, was a saying
among the Normans, at the field of Hastings,"
replied the pious divine Gilbert, "and many a
goodly castle survived its possessor, and many
a blow made a new baron; and as we of the
church wage war against Sathanas, I see not
why we should not reach the highest eminence,
as well as this pampered Saxon, who is now the
head over the Holy Church."

"If to lack piety is aught to be recom-
mended, thou and I will one day stand high in
the church," said Hilary, with a smile. "And
yet we have both stood fair in the fame of our
wood-craft, and could ever bestride a jennet,
and blow a mot, better than deliver an homily;
but *fortuna favet fatuis*, as was said long ago,
and it may be our turns at last."

"If there is truth in the Latin adage you
have just quoted, I think your reverence need not
despair," said Gilbert Foliot, who could not

resist having his joke, if even he had sacrificed
. the good will of his friend.

"You may also hope," answered Hilary, good
humoredly; "but there is no doubt of Queen
Eleanor——"

Their conversation was, however, suddenly
interrupted by the presence of King Henry,
who, followed by De Eynesford, burst into the
apartment like an enraged tiger; and without
regarding those present, at once gave vent to
his fierce passion. All, saving the excomuni-
cated knight, were ignorant of the cause of the
monarch's wrath, nor were they even aware of
the arrival of Becket, as they expected him to
make his appearance in all the pomp with
which he was wont to travel on public occasions,
and which we have described in a former
volume.

But when Henry entered with his countenance red with rage, his large blue eyes
blazing with almost an unnatural appearance;
his hands clenched, and his teeth set together;
every eye turned upon him in fear and astonishment. Nor were they in the least enlightened

as to the cause of his wrath, when they heard him exclaim, " This then is the reward for all my favours,—to be defied, set at nought! and bearded in my own palace, by the very man who hath wound himself into every secret of my heart. Oh God! that I should live to see myself thus trampled upon, and that too by—" He pressed his hands before his face, and leaning his burning brow against one of the cold pillars of the hall, remained several moments in silence, while the deep heaving of his broad chest only told of the painful struggle which was passing within.

Had a thunder-bolt fallen through the vaulted roof, and dashed one of the ponderous pillars into a thousand atoms, it could not have created more awe than at that moment reigned amid the assembled nobles. Eye looked up to eye in mute astonishment for information, and glanced from one countenance to another in silent wonder,—like a herd of deer, startled by a flash of lightning, that bound away, and then suddenly halt in some far forest glade, to gaze

around again in fearful amazement. So did
bishop and baron stare upon each other, until
at length all eyes centered upon William de
Eynesford; but he seemed to stand like a man
in a dream, so appalled had he been by the
bold bearing of Becket, and the furious rage of
the King.

At length Henry started suddenly from his
reverie, and exclaimed, in a voice which made
the arched roof ring again, " Earl of Leicester,
arrest the arch-traitor, Thomas à Becket instantly, and convey him to the dungeon! By
the face of God ! he shall not see the light of
heaven again until he hath done my bidding."

" Becket,—the Archbishop,—the Primate,—
a traitor,—arrest him,—the dungeon," &c. were
sounds that fell from all lips in almost every
imaginable tone, of wonder, triumph, disbelief,
doubt, and savage exultation; while the group
turned from one to another, with arm and head
thrown back ; and another volley of interjections
passed rapidly from tongue to tongue, as, " Holy
Virgin!" " Mother of Christ!" " Can this be?"

and so on: but not one either stepping up to obey the King's bidding, nor yet daring to reply, or interrogate him further on the matter. But during this sudden surprise, and before the Earl of Leicester had inquired where the Archbishop was to be found, Henry had changed his mind, and turning to an attendant, he said, "Tell the Archbishop of Canterbury, that we need not his presence at our banquet; he waits in the outer apartment." Then turning to the barons present, he added, "My Lords, you will pardon me for not sharing your festival to-day;" and without further explanation, he quitted the hall.

No sooner had the monarch withdrawn, than, like a parcel of schoolboys, who have some important tidings to impart to each other, and have been compelled to await their master's absence ere they dare venture to make them known; so did those grave bishops, and mailed barons huddle together; and instantly a score or two of tongues were let loose upon De Eynesford, who had scarcely breathing space left him, so closely was he hemmed in. Gilbert Foliot, the Bishop

of Hereford, an old enemy of Becket's, and the
Archbishop of York, who had himself been
intriguing for the Primacy, were among the
foremost to question De Eynesford respecting
Becket; and when the knight narrated the
whole of the interview, those right reverend
fathers could scarcely refrain from hugging
each other with delight, never remembering for
a moment the bold stand which the undaunted
Primate had made for their order, so much were
they overjoyed at the tidings of his quarrel with
the King.

The Bishop of Hereford, who was a little
fat red-faced personage, with a nose and chin
looking under and over his mouth, as if to give
the lie to abstinence, gave his reverend brother
divine a twitch on the arm, which made the
sleeve of his frock tremble in its stitches, and
led the way to a deep oriel window, whither he
was speedily followed by father Hilary, who
came up rubbing his hands and chuckling to
himself, and feeling as much delight as a miser,
who has paid away an often-tried and bad half-

crown. But it was not until they had obtained
that side of the huge oriel which screened
them from the observation of those in the hall,
that they ventured to give full vent to their feelings. Hilary of Chichester was as remarkable
for his thinness as the other for his corpulency.
And as Gilbert stood with his broad body to the
light, his hands resting on his thighs, and his
form half-bent, showing his teeth, and grinning
in silence at his right reverend brother, who
assumed the same attitude, they seemed like
light and shade personified, and rehearsing
the parts of clowns for some forthcoming mys-
tery, such as those grave gentry indulged in,
even at that remote period. After they had
grinned at each other for some time in silence,
and all but brought their bright shaven crowns
in contact, they seated themselves on the massy
oaken bench, which was fitted up to correspond
with the form of the window.

"It works," said Gilbert Foliot, rubbing his
course red hands together, then patting his
brother bishop on the shoulder.

" It does! it does! better than a miracle,"
answered Hilary, his long, thin, hungry face
looking like a sheep's head with a smile upon
it. " Queen Eleanor hath pitched upon a right
plan for her purpose; she has got them both into
purgatory."

" And it will be long ere I offer up a mass to
redeem one of them," said the red-nosed bishop;
" neither quotidian, nor month's mind,—anni-
versary or *abit*—but sooner set about to form
new masses to keep them there, were it once
their safe lodgment."

" May they not yet make matters up again?"
inquired Hilary. " What if Becket should
change his mind,—absolve this Kentish knight,
—give up his claim to the castle of Rochester
and other things,—where then go all the
Queen's plans?"

" To the strengthening of her next," replied
gross Gilbert with a knowing shake of the head.
" But all this, I tell thee, she has foreseen;
and thinkest thou, that if even the Archbishop
(oh, how that word sticks in my throat!) were to

do this, Henry would not at once begin to
reduce his power, that he might no more have
such cause of complaint? Aye, marry would he;
and pare away while there was aught left to
cut at, as you and I have often done at a haunch
of venison which we had provided during
Lent."

" But what if the King leaveth nothing but
the bone?" said hungry-looking Hilary; " it
will be but of little avail, I trow, the Queen
rewarding thee with the Primacy when it is
clean picked;—small share shall I have, too, for
aiding thee in thy plans."

" A straw for thy fears!" answered the pious
Gilbert; " I thought thou hadst known me too
well to fear that my conscience would boggle
at a stray form or two. Let Henry take mitre,
stole, and crook, so that he leaves me the flock
to pick; what care I if he be called the shepherd,
so that he winks at my entry into the fold."

" Thou sayest sooth, good brother," replied
Hilary with a grin; " it is but calling veal-
cutlets crimped cod, and keeping fish in thy

mind instead of flesh; and thou mayest satisfy both thy conscience and thy stomach at the same time, providing thou dost not let too many of the brethren put their hand into the same dish. But hark! I hear the clattering of trenchers; they are already preparing for the feast."

" Which I must not wait to partake of," said the bishop of Hereford; " for it is fitting that Eleanor should have early notice of what hath to-day befallen; so I will but get one of the attendants to bring me a few mouthfuls of food and a cup of wine, ere I set out again for Oxford."

Leaving the unholy hypocrites to eat their meal, and form their plots against the high-minded primate, we will turn for a few moments to the group seated at the huge tables in the centre of the hall; for the banquet has no claim to our attention, as we have already described a similar scene in our former volume. Although the feelings entertained by the party were not uttered in set speeches by the leaders,

as is the case in the present day; yet never on
the eve of any great political change in modern
times was party spirit more bitterly awake than
on that day in the hall of Woodstock. Even
the few who were well-wishers to Becket, were
compelled to sit in silence; for so bitter were
the invectives poured forth by the brutish
Norman barons over their wine, that for the
few to take his part, whose hearts were with
him, would have been tempting fifty daggers to
leap at once at their throats. All that rumour
had ever set afloat against the character of
Becket in former times, was on that day repeated; every one of his enemies remembered
something that told against him; while by
some strange oversight all his good deeds, and
knightly actions were forgotten. Men who had
held his stirrup, and waited at his table, who
had even with their own hands groomed his
favourite charger, and fed his choicest hounds,—
drank to the downfall of the son of the Saracen
slave; for they even raked up the memory of
the dead, to give a deeper colouring to their

hatred. Once only was his name vindicated by the Earl of Leicester, who, in reply to some doubt about his former valour, swore by one of his deepest oaths, that a braver knight never shivered a lance; and added, that although he hated him as a saint, yet he loved him as a soldier. But why dwell longer on the scene? it was such a one as is enacted every day; and although the state of mankind was then more unpolished, it was more sincere; and those ebullitions of feeling which the present forms of society, either keep down or make known more guardedly, were then daringly displayed, and instead of rankling long in the breast, were often quenched by bloodshed on the spot. For, be it remembered, that refinement of manners does not always better the human heart; no more than the removal of a wild and poisonous plant into a trim garden, changes its evil qualities; for the feelings of the savage are to be found even in civilized society.

CHAPTER IV.

This too much lenity
And harmful pity must be laid aside.
To whom do lions cast their gentle looks?
Not to the beast that would usurp their den.
Whose hand is that the forest bear doth lick?
Not his that spoils her young before her face.

SHAKSPEARE.

LEAVING Becket to cool his choler by a ride
through the park of Woodstock, we shall, for
a few pages, follow the king, from the time
that he so suddenly quitted the banquet hall.
Henry was a man of stormy passions, firm in
his friendships as most; but when once moved
to hatred, tearing on and crushing all beneath
him. It was not a trifling offence that could
change him; the wound must be deep ere he
would feel it, but once sent home to the heart,
the assailant was never again forgiven. Never for
a moment had the slanderous whispers which

were constantly circulating in the palace affected the king; but the more Becket's enemies
sought to lessen him in the monarch's esteem,
the closer did he rivet his friendship on every
public occasion: true he had ever found the
primate willing to serve him without hesitation,
and the mutual interchange of kindness between
them, had hitherto seemed to spring from the
esteem they held for each other. Henry felt
the unkindness of Becket deeply; his very
soul was pained, and when his anger had in
some measure subsided, there still rankled at
his heart a deep melancholy, a consciousness
that he had received injury from the man who
had long held undisputed sway in his bosom;
a man to whom every secret of his soul was
known; his most inmost thoughts and sincerest
opinions, which had never been divulged to any
other, for few men have more than one true
friend.

Writhing under these emotions, he left the
hall by a side-door, and pacing the long

gallery, entered the very apartment which
the primate had but a few moments before
quitted; but there he found no rest. In that
very room had they often caroused together :
there they had laughed and sung, pledged
each other in the huge goblets which still
glittered in the recesses; exchanged their
opinions about every one who moved in the
court; laid down their plans for humbling the
pride of one, and raising another; and often,
when the business of the state required their
presence, had they sat there laughing at each
other's wit; and if the historians of the age
belie them not, more than one fair lady has
shared their revels, whose lord was guarding
some distant fortress.

Henry gazed a moment around the apartment, and a deep sigh upheaved his broad breast,
as object after object met his eye, and reminded
him of bygone scenes. There hung the antlers
of a deer they had chased together, when they
outstripped all their followers, and were be-

nighted in the forest, and both weary and hungry, rested together under a broad oak until sunrise. Opposite were a couple of lances crossed, with which each had unhorsed three knights in the lists. Near to these hung a rich suit of chain armour, which Becket had brought over from France and presented to him. These and a hundred other similar things met the monarch's eye; and while his heart swelled for·a moment, his natural pride arose, and he summoned an attendant, and commanded him to strip the walls of all their ornaments.

Leaving the menial thus employed, he caught the sound of the voices assembled in the hall at the banquet, and was at no loss to conceive the cause of their hilarity; but the image of his favourite was not yet struck out of his affections, and he hurried across the court-yard, and passing the postern, crossed the moat in the same direction as that by which Rosamond escaped from Ugglethred. His foot once upon the greensward, he drew his short Anjou cloak, (which he had snatched up hastily, to cover the rich tunic) closely around him; and threading his way through the winding foot-paths in the coppices, unconsciously traversed the direction to the labyrinth. Onward he went through the entangling underwood, without pausing a moment to consider the course he was pursuing. The songs of the birds in the covert, the rich aroma of the trees, and the sweet fragrance that rose from a thousand wild flowers, were passed by disregarded ; nor did he once pause until he had gained an open glade, at the end of which rose the shaggy eminence covered with brushwood and creeping plants, that sheltered the abode of his fair mistress.

Rambling knee-deep amid the long grass and sweet summer-flowers, was seen the figure of Gamas Gobbo, his arms waving up and down like the motion of a bird's wings, while from his thick lips issued that loud buzzing sound, which we have before described, and as he chased the honey-bees from flower to flower, the poor idiot seemed to be one of the happiest of the human race.

The monarch stood gazing upon him in silence; and while he remembered the thousand cares which weighed upon a crown, and the painful emotions which he then felt, he almost wished that he too had been born an idiot, and left to run all summer long among the flowers. Gobbo was, however, too much engrossed in his favourite pleasure, to notice the monarch, and Henry entered the inlet of the labyrinth unobserved. As he threaded his way through the dark and intricate passages which we have already described; he felt as if he could gladly resign all the cares and splendour of a king, to dwell with the beloved being whom that solitude sheltered, and his conscience smote him when he reflected on what he had done; entailing misery upon one who was dearer to him than his kingdom, and feeding ambition on misery, to satisfy its hungry cravings. There was a weight upon his heart which he had never be-

fore felt; a load which he would fain get rid of;
a sinking of the spirits, which told him that,
although he was a king, his nature was weak
and feeble as that of another man's.

He passed the faithful minstrel Pierre de
Vidal, without exchanging a word, he was at
a loss what to say, for now he had no one to
whom he could pour forth his feelings, but
Rosamond. Henry of England had but one
true friend amid all his thousands of flatterers!
(since that he stood on terms of defiance with
Becket,)—had but one to whom he could un-
bosom himself, and she lived in a solitude, such
as his meanest serf would have spurned, and in a
reputation which the wife of any *Theow*, who
was chained to the soil would have blushed to
have borne.

Light are the ears of love; for slow and
faltering as was his footstep, Rosamond recognized its sound, and was on the turret-stair, ere
he had half ascended it.

" What ails my lord ?" said she, her lustrous

eyes instantly assuming a look of fear, and her whole countenance undergoing such a sudden change, as only a woman's features can wear when she is alarmed for the object of her love. "Speak to me, Henry," added she, chaining his neck with her fair arms, as she had done a thousand times before: "thou art not well, my love, or thou wouldst not look thus solemnly upon thy Rose."

He returned her fervent embrace in silence, and entering her chamber, sat down upon the richly carved bench which ran round the oriel. Rosamond seated herself beside him, and leaning upon his shoulder, gazed upon his countenance, which wore the strong marks of care and anguish, until her beautiful eyes filled with tears, and she again entreated him to tell her what had thus moved him.

"I am half jealous," said Rosamond, at length endeavouring to rally her spirits, and forcing herself to smile, "that your Highness grieveth for the absence of your favourite, the

Primate. Thou wert wont to be more cheeı-
ful when he shared thy company; was it not
so?" added she, looking tenderly into his face,
for she was unconscious of what had happened.

"Name him not," said Henry, in a voice
trembling with deep emotion; "he hath to-day
avowed himself mine enemy."

"I speak of Thomas à Becket, my Lord,"
continued Rosamond, thinking that the King
mistook her meaning,—"your bosom friend, and
not of your enemies."

"The same," replied the King briefly, and
rising from his seat, "thinkest thou that one
less than himself could have moved me thus?"

"Take it not so seriously," said Rosamond,
her tongue faltering beneath its utterance and
hope; "some word spoken in warmth, that
could have no ill meaning; some misunderstand-
ing which your cooler moments will explain.
Believe me, my liege, the Archbishop harboureth
no ill against you."

"Rosamond," said Henry, pausing suddenly

amid his hurried walk, and looking fixedly into
her countenance, " he has power over me, and I
fear him, not for my sake alone, so much as
thine own. I have kept nothing from him; he
is familiar with my most inmost thoughts. He
needeth but to speak, and Aquitaine, Poictou
and Anjou fly from my grasp, and Eleanor is
again mistress of these possessions. Would to
Heaven that they had ever remained in her
power ! But no," added he, pacing the apartment rapidly, " I will be the first to proclaim
my own villany. Thou shalt ride beside me,
and every knee bend, and every voice hail thee
as England's rightful Queen. I will not be
driven to render thee the justice I owe thee ; it
shall be an act of my own pleasure, thou shalt
share my power, as thou hast long done my heart.
To horse! Pierre de Vidal," he added, throwing open the casement, " spur for life and death
to our capital, and by sound of trumpet——"

  " Stay, my lord," said Rosamond, stepping
up and closing the casement, and motioning the

minstrel with her hand to withdraw, for he was
already about to ascend the turret stair ; " this
must not be,"' continued she, with a firmness
which Henry had never before seen her assume.
" Whatever your quarrel may have been with
the Primate, my liege, I know not, but I will
pledge myself for his honour, that he never
abuseth our secret, nor basely betrayeth the
trust your Highness hath placed in him."

" Ah! wilt thou too take the part of this
traitor !" exclaimed the King, his countenance
flushed with anger, and his large blue eyes
fixed upon her, as if they would pierce into her
very soul. " No! no!" added he, after a long
pause, his stern features gradually relaxing,
" thou knowest him not; thou hast not felt his
words since he became the ascetic churchman ;
thou hast not encountered his chilling glance;
thou only rememberest him as the common
friend to whom we imparted all our secrets,
when his conscience only leant to our bidding,
when I loved thee the more that thou didst

repeat his praises, and my heart was only shared by thyself and him. But now," continued he, with a bitterness of speech that made Rosamond start, " I hate him more than I did love him."

" What hath he done, my liege ?" inquired Rosamond, alarmed at the King's earnestness of manner, and fearing that matters were indeed serious while they thus excited him. " Assuredly he hath not erred beyond forgiveness?"

" Defied me!" replied Henry, in a voice of thunder, and hurrying up and down the apartment like a madman, while he spoke. " Set at nought my power, and refused to do my bidding,—declared himself King of the church, and, acknowledging no power above him but the Pope, dared me to oppose him ; cursed and excommunicated without my will; claimed castles and heritages for the church, and will ere long leave me but a crowned mockery, the mere shadow of a king, a puppet moved by the wires which he would manage. Oh! I could thrust my head into the earth, and bury myself for

shame when I think how foolish I have been.
I have bared my heart to him, and he hath
availed himself of all its weaknesses, and now
despiseth me. He found me a willing steed
to mount, patted and flattered me until he
seated himself upon my back; and now he
would shake the reins above my head, and spur
on until I become mad. Oh fool! that I was,
not to hearken to my nobles, and spurn the
Saxon slave when he came to lick my foot, ere
I had allowed him to bite me. No," added he,
again pausing, while the foam hung upon his
lips, and he stood erect in all his dignity, as if
he suddenly remembered that it was beneath a
king to be thus moved by a subject. "He
shall find me no lazy steer, to be fed until I am
sleek, then quietly submit myself to the yoke.
I will gore to death the first that dares to harness
me. Like a malignant comet, I will tread
fearlessly along my fiery course; and when I
have blazed out my time, leave a blank and
burnt-up desolation for a future age to marvel at."

he lion was at last aroused within him, and
he stood with his nostrils dilated, and his huge
chest thrown out, as if he would have dared the
shock of a thunderbolt; his pride had blazed
forth, and extinguished all pity.   Never did he
look more like a king : there was a fearful
majesty in his knit brow, clenched teeth, and
folded arms,—a look of daring decision: a
breathless and fearless resolution seemed to have
possessed him, and he stood like a giant secure
in his own power, as if he suddenly remembered that he need but turn round to rend those
who were pursuing him, his nerves seemed to have
become firm as iron.   Rosamond gazed upon him
in fear and astonishment ; never before had she
beheld him clothed in such stern dignity ; so
wrapt up in the iron mail of resolution, and
ready to meet the shock of all comers.   He
stood like a firm landmark on the shore of a
stormy sea, that bares its foundation before a
thousand breakers, and stands the bursting of
every billow unmoved.   His mind was firmly

made up, the molten iron of his passion shaped and hardened itself into a form, he resolved to maintain his dignity to the death, and never to forgive Becket while he breathed; and rigidly was that resolution kept.

Rosamond was the first to break that fearful silence, and her tongue faltered lest that she should again awake the sleeping tempest; as she thus spoke :—" I will not gainsay thee, my Lord, nor deign to offer aught in apology for what the Archbishop may have done; but still I dare to affirm that he is too honourable to take advantage of your secret respecting myself; and right loath should I be to make our marriage a stumbling-block over which your Highness might fall, and bring down with you all the thousands that have hitherto remained firm. While I stand innocent in the eyes of God, in your own mind, and my own conscience, I care but little for the opinion of others ; nor would I that dissension should be sown between yourself and your subjects in Aquitaine and Poictou, merely to make me that which I would avoid being. Your Queen," added she, her heart swelling as she spoke, "covets not that domestic quietude, which is all I crave for; as for name, and fame, and the world's opinion, they are but shadows that pass over the stream, without rippling its surface; they affect not the deep under-current that flows on unseen. No, believe me Henry," continued she, laying her hand gently upon his folded arms, " I have no wish to cope with my dangerous rival. I am happy in the possession of thy love, and——" She was about to proceed, when a child bounded into the apartment, and looking into Henry's face with his smiling blue eyes, exclaimed, " Father!" and seizing his mother's hand,—with the other he grasped the skirts of the monarch's rich tunic.

For a moment, the King gazed affectionately upon the child, and he ran his fingers through the silky clusters of its hair, then cast a sad fond look upon the countenance of Rosamond,

and passing his hand over his brow, while he
turned away to hide his emotion, exclaimed
in a sorrowful voice: "Alas! I am doomed to
bring misery upon all who are dear to me; even
the innocence of childhood is not free from the
curse which attends me. No," added he, "I
will yet be honest to myself. I will to Rome,
and procure a divorce from Eleanor. I was
entrapped by the wily traitress; even the dotard
Louis spurned her from his bed. I will not
leave the child to be pointed at with the finger
of scorn when I am dead; but make him what
he is, the rightful heir to my kingdom. Men
shall bow before him, and acknowledge him
their liege lord, and not pass him by as a
son of base birth. He shall be sought out,
and courted by the Norman nobles, and not
shunned as their inferior. It shall not be said,"
continued he, again, carried away with his
feelings, " that a breath of Becket's gave him
royalty: I will lead him forth of mine own
accord, and he shall stand in the midst of them;

until, like young eagles which are taught to gaze upon the sun, they all become familiar with his countenance."

But Rosamond again uplifted her gentle voice, and by her persuasive arguments prevented the irresolute monarch from accomplishing his intention, preferring even peace to her own fair fame, and the reputation of her children.

So on a breath revolve the mighty affairs of this world. The sound of a few trumpets, and the shouts of a score or two voices would have made Rosamond a queen ; and her child William, surnamed Longsword, the King of England. But they were silent, and the one in exchange was doomed to bear the title of concubine, and the other to be called the son of a harlot; when even a word of Becket's could have made him the progenitor of a long and glorious line of kings.

CHAPTER V.

I am too high-born to be property'd,—
To be a secondary at controul,
Or useful serving-man, and instrument
To any sovereign.

But when we in our viciousness grow hard,
(O misery on't) the wise gods seal our eyes ;
In our own filth drop our clear judgments ; make us
Adore our errors ; laugh at us, while we strut
To our confusion.

SHAKSPEARE.

WE left the high-minded and angry primate riding at full speed through the park of Woodstock, chafed to the very soul at the thoughts of being dismissed from the palace; when, if he had but made up his mind to have started a minute earlier, he might have saved himself much painful humiliation. To a proud soul like Becket's, these feelings were maddening. " To be ordered away like a beggar," thought

he, as he galloped through the chase, as if it
was infected by a plague,—" and I too the
Primate of England; the head of the church;
high in my episcopal situation, as Henry is on
his throne!—the thought is not to be borne.
The very grooms at the gate cast a grim smile
of triumph at me as I passed. No, I will hold
no terms with him longer; but will grasp my
pastoral crook as firmly as he does his sceptre,
and invest the church with more power than ever
belonged to the crown. Not a right that I can
claim for it shall escape me. I will show
this overbearing king with whom he has to
deal."

Such, and even thoughts more severe against
the King, passed through the excited mind of
Thomas à Becket, as he rode at full gallop
along the winding road, which was here and
there overhung with the arms of gigantic oaks,
and the huge branches of aged and stately
elms. Neither did he for a moment turn his
thoughts to his faithful attendant, Gryme, so

much had anger overpowered all his calmer reflections, and carried away, at one fell swoop, all those remembrances of prayer and penance, and those severe lessons of self-denial and humiliation which he had so long practised. Be it remembered, however, that from the time he was created Archbishop, he had so schooled his mind, as to firmly believe that it was his duty to sacrifice everything for the good of the church; that his duty to Heaven, the Pope, and his own conscience, were of more consideration than aught on earth beside; and that he had carried this duty to the very verge of severity, making even no allowance for those who did not deem it so essential to play the tyrant for the love of religion. His zeal had in a great measure eaten him up; and he tortured both his body and mind to great excess, playing the part of devil to himself here, that he might prevent the horned authorities from tormenting him hereafter; and forgetting that among his baldheaded brethren of the church, there were very

few who had done so many unclerical deeds as
himself. There was in fact a pride about his
piety,—a painful regularity in all his forms of
prayer and penance, mingled with a kind of
haughty sternness, which was rooted in his soul,
and from which sprang all his ambition. His
hair-shirt was of the coarsest, and he never
moved but it gave him torture; but over this he
wore the richest robes of office, palliums of
costly velvet, ornamented with gold, and bor-
dered with the richest minever. His food was
of the plainest, such as even a beggar would
have refused; but it was brought to him in
vessels of silver or gold, richly embossed; and
he would often take his meal of coarse bread
and water; whilst his favourite hound was
regaling on a rich repast of cold venison at his
feet. Such a man was Thomas à Becket; born
to be a leader in whatever station of life he
might be thrown; and if there have been holier
men elevated to the primacy, there never was
one who stuck up more firmly for its dignity.

If he wavered, it was but for a moment; like some goodly ship, staggered by an unexpected hurricane, that reels and dips her white sails for an instant in the surges, then rises buoyant and erect, to trample upon the thunder of a thousand billows.

While the Archbishop was riding at such a furious rate through the shady and forest-like paths of the park, Gamas Gobbo chanced suddenly to emerge from a thick underwood, and darting across the road with his loud buzzing noise, in chase of a large brown bee, he startled the primate's steed, which, without abating its force, wheeled instantly on one side, and ran its head with such force against the stem of an enormous oak, that both horse and rider came instantly to the ground. The dignity of the Prelate was not at all enhanced by being thus suddenly precipitated headlong into a thicket of brambles; nor did it add to the nobleness of his figure to see him crawl out on all fours, his hands covered with moist clay,

E 5

and his rich riding-cloak here and there be-
smeared with the same material. But what
added to the drollery of the scene, was the
figure of Gobbo jumping up and down in the
middle of the road, humming and waving his
skinny arms,—now turning his yellow eyes upon
the Primate,—then watching some heavy bee
as it flew buzzing to a neighbouring woodbine.
Nor was the sudden and unexpected shock
passed by without having an influence on the
mind of Becket; for it did more for the moment
to abate his anger against the king, than any
hour's argument Gryme could have introduced;
and for the first time he seemed to become
conscious of the absence of his attendant.

Who, however, should come up at the
moment, but Gilbert Foliot, the bishop of
Hereford, riding at full speed on his way to
carry tidings of Becket's quarrel with the King
to Eleanor; he having taken a different turning
of the wood, and outridden Gryme. With
many a low bow, and sentence of sympathy,

uttered in bad Latin, did this hoary old hypocrite alight, and giving the reins of his palfrey to Gamas, proceeded to offer his services to the primate. Meantime, Gobbo, idiot as he was, had observed several flies hovering around the wallets of the bishop, and knowing by a kind of instinct, that there was something more attractive than legends of the saints, or missals to draw them hither, he, without delay, commenced a search, and having drawn out the corner of an enormous pasty, he gave so high a jump, and so loud a buzz, that he frightened the horse of the poor bishop, and away it rushed at a bound into the thicket, and was instantly out of sight.

The right reverend rider at that moment had his back turned towards Gobbo, and with hands outspread and body bent forward, was making an offer of his steed to the primate, and had just delivered himself of some holy saw; at the end of which came in his "*Laus Deo*," for the miraculous preservation of Christ's representative, and vowing how many prayers should be offered up at the abbey of Hereford,— when his ear was arrested by the rushing of his steed through the underwood, and his eye instantly alighted upon the huge corner of the pasty which Gobbo (his mouth full) was flourishing in one hand, while his other arm kept up an incessant circular motion, and he buzzed at his highest pitch of voice with delight.

Even Becket could scarcely keep his solemn and noble looking countenance, as he beheld the ponderous prelate make a rush at Gobbo, and forgetting all his protestations of piety, he exclaimed, " May the curse of the foul fiend alight upon thy ugly carcase !"   But the idiot was not to be thus caught; for, waiting until the huge bishop was just within reach of him, he sprang aside like an elastic branch, and down tumbled his reverence, face foremost, into a spot where a cow but an hour before had lain quietly chewing her cud.

When this dirty pillar of the church stood bolt upright, the primate of England could not refrain from laughing aloud; and had King Henry by chance have come up at that moment, the calendar would have numbered a martyr less, and the Cathedral of Canterbury been shorn of the gifts of ten times ten thousand pilgrims; for the king would have thrown himself into the primate's arms, and the walls of the palace of Woodstock would again have rung with the old familiar sounds of their laughter. Never had divine a more unclerical appearance than the reverend father of Hereford. His huge red nose looked as if it was cased in the very darkest of Roman cement; and his broad double chin bore no inapt resemblance to the newly-upturned furrows of a plough-field, while every crease in his bagging cheeks and deep eye-pits seemed laid in, in contrast to the crimson bits that here and there peeped out; he looked like a bishop dead-coloured, or an old portrait newly touched, at the door of a picture-cleaner's. Becket, who was well acquainted with the character of the bishop, could not resist the temptation of venturing a few sarcasms at his expense, as he was not ignorant of the ill-will which he bore him.

" Pity, holy father, that thou shouldst meet with such a sad mishap," said the primate, his countenance, in spite of all the sympathy he attempted to throw into it, assuming a sneer; " when thou wert in the act of conferring kindness upon one of the church, and not, like Saul, riding forth to persecute the children of Christ."

The bishop, who at that moment was stooping down, and wiping his face upon the skirt of his mantle, paused suddenly, and cast a peculiar glance upon Becket; for his conscience smote him, when he remembered, that the very cause of his journey, was to hasten the downfall of the primate ; and he began to suspect from the allusion couched in his remarks, that Becket knew the secret of his mission, and he stammered forth in reply the following: "The evil-one, most holy and reverend father, it is written, shall have power over us, and when we think that we stand securely, cometh in some form or other and causeth our fall. And even as the devils were cast out, and entered into the herd of swine, so do I believe that Sathanas himself hath taken possession of that imp who now standeth, gibbering, and buzzing, and mocking us, as if he delighted in our overthrow. Had I not forgotten my flask of holy water, I would even here exorcise and cast him out."

"Methinks the holy work may yet be done," said Becket, " for but now I observed the idiot, or fiend, whichever he may be, take out a flask from your wallet, and it doubtless containeth that which your reverence bemoaneth the loss of."

"Blessed St. Dunstan! it is even so," exclaimed Gilbert, turning his eyes to where Gobbo stood with the leathern bottle to his lips, taking a hearty draught, after having

finished his pasty, for the flask had been filled
with excellent Rhenish by the Cellarer at the
palace;—"it is even so, and he swalloweth it, as
if it were but the common flowing of the brook,
when it was drawn from the well of St. Winifred,
and a hundred paternosters repeated over it,
every one of which was numbered with a bead."

"I fear me," replied the primate, "that they
have prayed without their beads, or your reverence may have been mistaken in the flask,
seeing that the idiot smacketh his lips together,
and rolleth up his ears, as if he was enjoying
the true flavor of wine or strong drink, rather
than the holy water of the well of St. Winifred."

"Troweth your holiness, that I journey
abroad, laden with forbidden drink?" said the
bishop, uplifting his dirty hands, and rolling up
the white of his eyes, which showed the more
clearly from the dingy colour of his countenance;
"or that in the very same mail in which I carry a
relic of the blessed St. Gertrude, the homilies

of the holy Ambrose, and that sacred missal
which was dropped into the abbey of Hereford
by a holy hand, in which the face of the virgin
is to be seen,—even as she looked when upon
earth, and as she now showeth herself to her
servants here below, with stars on her head,
the moon beneath her feet, and an infant upon
her knee;—wherein there is Moses with his
horns of gold, Michael grasping his spear, the
blessed St. Peter with his keys, St. John with
his chalice, and St. James with his shells;—
where the angels are girding the loins of Thomas
of Aquin, and the sacred spider is spinning her
web to conceal Athanasius, while the merciful
Anthony of Padua, with his mallet, is breaking
the heads of heretics, or preaching to a holy
host of fishes, who are bowing their heads, as if
to say Amen. Oh, it is a strange volume, and
a blessed volume, and hath been known to close
its leaves, when aught of evil hath been near it;
nor will it open unless first sprinkled with holy
water: then its leaves shine like the candle of

Genovefa, or the eyes of the rats around St. Gertrude; yea even bright as the glance of Anthony of Egypt, when he frightened away the evil one."

During the lying narrative of the bishop, Becket who appeared to be attentively listening, had kept his eye fixed on Gamas Gobbo, who having amused himself long enough with the leathern bags, at length threw them down, and bounded off after two bees, that went humming leisurely along above the wild flowers, as they were retreating to their hives, for the sky was heavy and lowering. No sooner did the primate observe this, than he sprang hastily forward, and seizing the half-filled flask with one hand, he grasped the bishop's wallet with the other; and applying the mouth of the leathern-bottle to his lips, was soon convinced that the holy water from the well of the blessed St. Winifred was the oldest rhenish from the cellars of Woodstock. And just as his brow had become clouded, and was about to charge the bishop as

the chief of liars and the basest of hypocrites,
his reverence, probably anticipating what would
follow, shot off at once into the thicket, exclaiming, " Yonder is my palfrey, I will be with your
reverence anon."

The first thought of the archbishop, was to
throw the flask at the head of Gilbert Foliot, as
he retreated, but from this he desisted, and proceeded to examine the contents of his reverence's
wallet. Far be it from us to belie those holy
men of old, but true it is that there did fall from
between the leaves of an old illuminated missal,
a slip of parchment which was addressed to
the bishop of Hereford, and subscribed by an
holy abbess, living in the said shire. And could
our readers have peered over the shoulder of
the primate, and deciphered those ancient
letters, they would have discovered, how a
certain postern had been left open for several
nights, by the holy abbess, and how a devout
nun had been constantly on the look-out for his
reverence; that the finest capons had been slain,

and the best wine kept in readiness among the sacred relics, where no one ventured to peep, saving on rare occasions, but herself.

Becket glanced his eye angrily over the document, as he muttered to himself, "No marvel that the Church of Christ hath fallen to this low estate, while such wolves in sheep's clothing have entered the fold. But I will cast them out," continued he, drawing the hood of his mantle over his shaven crown; for big drops of rain were already falling, and a huge dark cloud which had long hovered over the eastern side of the wide park slowly moved along, and now blackened that part of the sky under which the Archbishop seemed to stand. He attempted, but in vain, to raise his fallen steed; the animal groaned heavily and bled profusely from the chest, for in falling it had alighted upon the sharp stem of a jagged hawthorn. Gamas Gobbo flew to the Prelate's aid, and displayed much skill in endeavouring to raise the horse, but their united efforts were of no avail; so the

idiot only pointed to the wound, gave a louder
buzz than usual, shook the rain which was now
falling in torrents from his rugged and elfin
locks, then rushed for shelter under a neighbouring oak; the broad branches of which
covered many a yard of green grass and entangling underwood. The proud Prelate was
compelled to follow the example of the idiot,
and seating himself upon the mossy stem of the
gigantic tree, he drew the hood closer around
his head; folded his flowing and costly garments more tightly around him, and sat watching the heavy shower that seemed to smoke
along the earth, until his countenance again
assumed its former sternness, and his thoughts
once more reverted to his interview with Henry.
For a few moments the eyes of Gamas were
fixed upon the thoughtful countenance of the
Prelate; then he threw himself on the wet
greensward, only half arising as some heavy
bee now and then blundered past to seek for
shelter, or clapping his hands together to scare

some wet-winged songster, that shot by in silence to the thicket. So they sat, the idiot without a care, ever and anon drawing some bee from his bosom, and extracting from it the honey bag; while the heart of Becket was steeped in the bitterness of wormwood and gall, as his pride arose while contemplating the humility he had undergone; remembering that but an hour before he stood highest in the favour of his king; but was now, like the houseless beggar, compelled to shelter under the green boughs, or journey a-foot through the wet paths of the park with the sheeted rain teeming upon him. But he was aroused from these thoughts by the sound of hoofs, as Gryme, with his face buried in the folds of his mantle and drenched to the skin, appeared.

CHAPTER VI.

Let the great gods
That keep this dreadful pother o'er our heads,
Find out their enemies now. Tremble, thou wretch ;
That hast within thee undivulged crimes
Unwhipped of justice. Hide thee, thou bloody hand !
Thou perjured, and thou simular man of virtue,—
Caitiff, to pieces shake.

King Lear.

THE delay of the faithful monk was owing to
his ignorance of the paths of the park ; for, as
we have before remarked, its enclosure was
comparatively recent, and as it contained nearly
ten times the space of ground which it stood
upon a century ago, many parts still bore its
ancient and forest-like appearance. When,
however, Gryme had alighted and cast his eye
upon the dying steed, and glanced at the wet
drapery of the Prelate, his conscience smote
him for the delay, and he gazed upon his master

with a look of pity and self-reproach. Becket
returned his glance tenderly and without anger,
and he was the first to break the painful silence
by saying, " Thou seest we are already schooling
ourselves for further trials, Gryme; we have
sought shelter where the dun deer herd together,
and are waiting with a like patience until the
tempest passes away."

" Steed foundered, and garments drenched!
and sheltering in the wild underwood with an
idiot!" said Gryme, almost unconsciously to
himself; " Arise, my dear master, and let us
return to the palace. Hark! how the thunder
is muttering in the distance; and see how the
edges of yonder dark cloud are already fringed
with lightning: arise! and let us begone ere
the storm comes armed in all its fury."

" Not a step," said Becket, springing up like
a war-horse at the sound of the trumpet. " Return, saidst thou?" continued he, moving rapidly
under the lowest bough which his high head
touched and brought down a shower, as if from

a water-spout; " no, not if it were midnight;
and if I were doomed to make this wet
grass my couch, and every tree in the chase
were to shiver around me, struck by the pros-
trating bolts of Heaven! Gryme, thou didst
but jest with me," added he, fixing his eyes
upon the attendant, nor shifting his glance,
although the red lightning at that moment
flashed across his noble countenance, and made
the whole shadow of the oak, under which they
stood, one broad blaze of light. Then again
broke forth the deep-throated thunder, and
shook every tree in the vast park as it went
growling along under the gloomy and threatening
vault of heaven. The affrighted idiot threw
himself flat upon the earth, with his face
downward, and Gryme drew the folds of his
mantle closer around him ; while Becket alone
stood bare-headed and erect amid the storm, as
if he was unconscious of its fury.

" It must not be," muttered the monk, as if
suddenly recollecting himself, and instantly un-

loosing the grey mantle from his shoulder to throw around the Primate; " hasten then to Oxford, in Heaven's name ! for the day threateneth to close darkly; thou canst bestride mine own palfrey, and I will journey beside thee on foot; or wait here until the storm abates, if thou wilt not return to the palace."

" To the palace I will not return," said Becket, placing the mantle again upon the shoulder of his faithful follower, and with his own hands fastening the loop; "wouldst thou have the Primate of England kneel down to crave shelter like a very beggar; to go back cringing like a spiritless cur that hath been spurned by the foot of his master. No! we will journey on our way together when the fury of the tempest hath subsided. I can better brook the pelting of the storm, than the cold and contemptuous glance of the King. He shall not say, that I humbled myself at his gates; or was ushered by his grooms into the galleries to wait among his falconers and keepers of his kennels, which the hurricane will drive homeward."

"Patience! holy father," replied Gryme, veiling his eyes from the glaring lightning; "forget not those pious lessons which you have ever taught the brethren of your order: remember that anger is but feeding the flames; that Christ forgave his enemies ; and that, however high the wrath of the King might be kindled, his nature is forgiving; and that his pity and remembrance of former friendship could again be awakened in this hour of danger, when the very heavens are pouring forth their rage."

The monk meant kindly to his master, and was naturally a peace-maker; but unfortunately, like too many others who are full of good intentions, he too often widened the breach in place of closing it; and the words *pity* and *danger* fell harshly on the ears of the high-souled Prelate; and like a proud steed, which the rider thinks to check by plunging his spurs into its side, instead of handling the reins judiciously, he instantly began to rear and plunge, and show greater symptoms of restlessness than ever.

" Pity! danger !" echoed the Primate, bridling up as he repeated the words; and disregarding the loud thunder which now burst forth like the roaring of a thousand lions, while the heavy rain, which had by this time penetrated through every branch of the broad and deep-foliaged oak, caused Gamas Gobbo to arise from his saturated couch, and huddle closer to the stem of the tree. " Gryme, I have looked upon death; in the iron ranks of battle we have met each other face to face : danger and I have become companions ; we have stood many a brunt together on the stormy sea, and amid the combat on land; we have confronted each other so often, that we have become familiar, and have long ago met without fear. No; I would sooner plant myself as a mark for the merciless lightning upon the highest oak

that towers above us, than seek to share the
pity of the King. I tell thee, that ere this
he hates me, since that he hath found I am
marble under his hand instead of wax, and will
not take his impress,—will not barter the church
of God for his favour. Pity! saidst thou?"
continued he, scattering the rain from the
long grass as he moved to and fro in his excitement, unconscious of his situation; " as
soon believe that the deep ocean roars in pity
for those it has devoured,—that the wolf, gorged
to excess, seeks its cave to mourn over the
victim whose bones it has crunched ;—that the
midnight lightning came but to guide the
traveller it struck dead,—as that I should
awaken his pity. No!" added he with energy, and
instantly checking his rapid strides; " I am beyond the reach of his pity, and will teach him to
fear me. He hath set his foot upon an angry wave,
that he thought to hasten shoreward; forgetting that it would roll back to the deep from
whence it sprung, and bring with it a thousand

heavier breakers. The thunder of Rome is only
dormant; and will shake the wide welkin when
it is aroused; and mine," continued he,
speaking in his loudest tone, " is a voice that
can bid it awaken !"

As he spoke, he stood with his tall figure
erect, and his arm waving aloft, while his brow
was flushed with passion, and his ample drapery
fell around him in graceful folds; and scarcely
had the words left his lips when, as if at the
bidding of a mighty magician, the red-winged
lightning gave a deeper crimson to his countenance, and filled every avenue of the park
with flames, as if a million blazing banners had
waved at his beck, then again became suddenly
folded. Then came the deep thunder in one
fearful and continuous peal that seemed as if it
would split the sky asunder; while it shook the·
firm foundations of the earth; and the rain
clattered down like mountain-torrents, as if the
windows of heaven were again opened, and the
desolating deluge once more poured down upon
the world.

Gamas Gobbo gave a loud shriek, and clung
to the mantle of the archbishop in fear, and in
another instant, the form of Gilbert Foliot
was seen brushing aside the underwood as
he approached with a terror-stricken countenance, calling upon the name of every saint
for protection, and vowing to offer up candles
and masses, and to amend his crimes, in a
breath.   Even Gryme faltered beneath the
mighty uproar, and took up his beads, while
his lips moved rapidly as he ran over some
remembered prayer.   Becket alone stood unmoved: his deep and fiery eye kindled as if
with some sublime emotion.   While he gazed
upon the dark and angry sky, not a symptom
of fear settled upon his countenance; but he
stood like the statue of some god that has
bared his marble front before a thousand
thunders, and wrapped the lightning around
him like a mantle.   Nor did his countenance
change, until his eye alighted upon the trem-

bling form of the Bishop of Hereford; then
it assumed a look of dignified rebuke, beneath
which the hypocrite quailed, as his teeth
chattered again between cold and fear, for
he was drenched to the very skin.

"Miserable sinner!" said Becket, his anger
having in some measure passed away, while
his thoughts were absorbed for the few moments
in contemplating the fearful grandeur of the
tempest: "it becomes thee well to tremble
before the dreaded wrath of the Omnipotent,
thou who hast grown grey in crime, and bent
thy knees so long in mockery before the Most
High. Now doth thy conscience torture thee.
Get thee into some cavern, and there brood over
thy crimes, until repentance hath dug furrows
into thy cheeks, and obliterated the marks of
thy gross feeding. Think over the hours thou
hast wasted with that godless abbess, until thy
brow becomes wrinkled with fasting and prayer,
and remorse makes hollow thy eyes. Thou
hast too long grown fat upon lies, and fallen

asleep, dreaming over thy deceits for the morrow. Thou art one of those plague-spots which spreads like a rotting damp over the church, and would, in the end, eat its way through pillar and shrine, until the whole edifice was consumed."

"Have compassion upon him, holy father," said Gryme, who felt moved when he beheld the prelate bowed to the earth, and heaving forth piteous groans: "remember that we all are sinners, and that if we extend not our mercy to the fallen brethren on earth, we cannot look for it from the blessed saints in heaven, who are ever pleading for our infirmities."

"Thou knowest him not," said Becket sternly; "he is one of those who sheltereth his sins under his seeming sanctity, and is in heart more wicked than he who would rob the church of its sacred relics. The swineherd who eats of the mast which he shakes down for his hogs, and shareth at night their lair, is too good to harbour with such as he is.

Oh God!" exclaimed he, lifting up his countenance to heaven, while the descending light
which fell from between two masses of clouds,
gave a softness to his features and a radiance
to his bald crown, not unlike the light which
the old masters throw around their pictures of
the apostles; " how long wilt thou slumber
ere thou comest forth in all thy glory and all
thy vengeance, to purify the temple with the
fire of thy wrath, and drive from it all that
is unclean. Thou shakest the earth with the
thunder of thy terror, and uprootest the huge
oaks on the highest hills with the echo of thy
voice. Oh! shake the souls of those who
mock thee with their lips, while their hearts
are far from thee. Let them not rest until,
amid darkness and solitude, long fastings and
fervent prayers; flooding tears and deep groans;
they have worked out their repentance, in
sincerity, in fear and trembling and breathless
awe. How long shall the shrines of the Saints
be bowed to in mockery, and the Holy Virgin

invoked by those whose breath is burning with impure passions, and whose eyes are inflamed through keeping up their drunken vigils. Bow then the heavens in thy wrath, and come down and make the uttermost ends of the earth tremble, until every soul falls like the darkness at thy feet, and every knee bends until it grows to the ground. Send forth thy voice like the sounding of chariots upon the hills; let there be within their souls a voice of battle and of shouting, until despair, like the blackness of darkness, falls and is felt, and hope only breaks like the morning after a long night of sorrowful repentance."

While the archbishop thus proceeded, unconscious of what was going on around, Gilbert Foliot made his escape, for he could better bear the wet and cold of the underwood, than listen to these terrible enunciations. Gryme, however, harkened with bowed head, and uplifted hands, and, although the language of the prelate re-

sembled in a great measure such as was uttered
by the fanatics of a later day, yet strange was
the effect it sometimes produced, on the rude
auditors of that age.

The storm had by this time abated, and
Gamas Gobbo was the first to avail himself of
the calm, for the rich aroma that followed the
shower, (and which all must have inhaled who
have wandered in the solitudes of nature,) was
soon felt by the idiot, and he stood, like the
wild ass in Job, snuffing up the air; until bee
after bee broke forth; then away he bounded
his arms uplifted with the undulatory motion of
a bird flying, and he buzzed his gentlest notes,
as he shot into the thicket.

Becket mounted the horse of the monk, and
rode on at a gentle pace, while Gryme walked
beside him, and they journeyed along in silence
to Oxford, where they stayed that night, and
afterwards by easy stages returned to Canterbury. It was late before Gilbert Foliot reached
the palace with his tidings; and great was the

disappointment of his reverence, when he learnt
that some other messenger had outstripped him
several hours ; nor was this the greatest calam-
ity, for he was too late for the evening meal ;
and while he ate his morsel apart by the huge
fire, where he sat to dry his garments, his
conscience gave him sundry twinges, for he now
found himself completely at the mercy of the
primate, and well knew that, if dealt with according to his deserts, he should make but a
sorry figure. But we must leave him, for he
hath but little to do with our story.

CHAPTER VII.

Think not I love him, though I ask for him ;
'Tis but a peevish boy :—yet he talks well ,
But what care I for words? yet words do well,
When he that speaks them pleases those who hear.
                                        SHAKSPEARF.

IT was on the morning following the storm, that
Pierre de Vidal left the labyrinth to wander in the
secluded paths of the park ; for the remains of
the old forest-like solitudes had a charm for the
minstrel, which was all the sweeter when he
had Maud for a companion. He threaded his
way with folded arms and measured step along
the winding avenues, which in some places
skirted the banks of the Glyme, then wound
with many a picturesque meander deeper into
the neighbouring thickets. The brow of the

minstrel was overclouded with thought; and
although his dark eyes now and then became
lighted up with their natural and piercing brilliancy; yet it was only as some beautiful object
in nature presented itself; and the same moody
look, and melancholy gait were again unconsciously resumed. It was not long, however,
before Maud made her appearance, leading by
the hand the child of her mistress, and the son
of King Henry, and who was afterwards celebrated as William Longsword; for he even
rivalled the acknowledged, but scarcely more le-
gitimate Cœur de Lion, in the weighty weapons
which he in after-life wielded. There was a
bewitching look about Maud as she approached
in her blue tunic, her ample hood thrown back,
and her clustering hair bound with its neat
leathern band, and falling in graceful curls over
her gorget. Nor was there many a prettier foot
to be seen, than that which, encased in its plain
but neat sandal, and showing between the
thongs the dashing hose of deep scarlet, came

tripping through the dew and the daisies. She approached the minstrel with one of her sweetest smiles; and when, instead of receiving the customary salute which her pouting lips seemed to covet, she was only accosted with " good morrow to thee, fair Maud," she jerked her haughty head back until every ringlet seemed to dance again, and replied, " Good morrow, Master Vidal, an' that be all your greeting."

" Pardon me, my dearest Maud !" said the minstrel, drawing her beautiful face towards him, and imprinting a fervent kiss upon her lips; " I am ill at ease this sweet summer morning. This quarrel between my Royal Master and the Archbishop hath somewhat moved me. I know their unbending natures; and fear me that the rent is too wide to be made up in haste. How fares it with our gentle mistress ?"

" But indifferently," replied Maud, with a deep sigh; " she was wont to call the Primate her

father, ever since that fearful night you so well
wot of, when the villain Ugglethred———"

"Enough! enough! Maud," said the minstrel, grasping the hilt of the dagger in his
belt; "I know it all; and have not forgotten
how ill I kept my guard. But I have notched
my tally; and will not fail to compare the
reckoning whenever he crosses my path. Hush!
didst thou not hear a rustling in the underwood?"

"It was but the rushing of a stag which
William startled with his headless shaft," replied Maud; "you may blame yourself for
teaching him to handle such weapons; he
hath shot out the eyes of half the saints in
the painted window, and cracked more skulls
than St. Anthony of Padua ever did with his
mallet. And now he is off into the thicket
to rouse some hart from his harbour. Hang
the scape-grace! let him run until he is
weary; I see Gamas Gobbo is with him, and
have no fear of his safety."

"See what a golden green the sunlight throws upon yonder glade," said Vidal, disregarding the latter part of the damsel's speech; "and now the white stems of the birches look like the clearest and brightest of marble pillars, overhung with emerald, or trellised like the roofless columns that stand mocking the sunshine of azure-vaulted Italy. But thou likest not to hear me name these things, Maud; thou carest not for the poetry of the earth; and yet thou lovest flowers, the spring and summer, moonlight and starlight, the song of the nightingale and the murmuring of the waters of the Glyme. Dost thou not, dearest?"

"Marry do I," replied Maud; "but I love my fair mistress better than all these, and marvel at thee talking of such things, when thou knowest that she will need all our vigilance, the more that the primate will be absent from her; for thou knowest that he loved her like his own daughter."

" I love her too," said the minstrel ; "and would shed my heart's blood in her service ; the archbishop could do no more."

" But thou hast not said so much in her praise of late," said Maud ; " thou wert wont to extol her beauty, and compare her voice to all sweet sounds. Thinkest thou I should love thee the less didst thou praise her the more ?" added she, leaning fondly upon Vidal's shoulder.

"But thou didst say that there were eyes bright as her own," answered the minstrel, throwing his arm around her waist, and looking affectionately into her face ; "and when I said that she never spoke but in so soft a strain, that like the sweetest music it made us either smile or weep ; thou didst say that there were others could speak as softly when they were well pleased, and then keptest silence until we gained the avenue of the old oak-wood. When I said that there was something in her countenance which I could look upon until I grew aged, for the longer I gazed the more beauties I discovered; or ere I could name one, another arose that seemed to outvie the former; didst thou not unloose mine arm from thy waist, and bound away, without even giving me good even?"

" I did," answered Maud, bending lower her lovely head, that the minstrel might take tribute from her sweet lips for her misdeeds.

" Thou saidst rightly, dear Maud," continued Pierre de Vidal, suddenly recollecting himself, and unloosing his hold; "this is no time for dalliance, we must up and be doing, if we would serve those whom we love. I heard the king pacing the court-yard yester-even in the Palace of Woodstock, and vowing what means he would take to humble the Primate; and he was surrounded by those who are neither lovers of our gentle mistress nor of ourselves, but men who are often in close consultation with the crafty Eleanor."

" I understand not their policy, as I have heard thee call it," answered Maud; "but I know that there are many evil-minded men who are ever ready to raise themselves by another's downfall; and although the haughty Archbishop doth question me oftener about my aves, and credos, and paternosters, than he was wont to do when the gay Chancellor, yet my fair mistress hearkeneth to the same advice, and she is much wiser than myself. But somehow I cannot rock our youngest child asleep so soon by singing a *placebo,* as when I troll forth an old Saxon cradle-song; and methinks, for children, holy songs and anthems are useless, and might be reserved until they become of fitting age to understand them. But I must away, and seek yonder runaway boy, or Gamas Gobbo will be stinging him again with his bees: it was but the other day that his little fingers were swelled to double their size, and all through practising Gobbo's plan of taking out the honey-bag."

"Thou needest not to hurry," replied the minstrel, "I heard his voice but now in the thicket. But say, how is it that the lady Rosamond hath so seldom been abroad of late; she

was wont to take her walks oftener, and I had
hopes of making her a lover of the divine art;
she hath of late hung down her head like a
violet bowed beneath the dew. What new
grief hath befallen her?"

"None, but such as fall upon our royal master," answered Maud with a sigh; "I thought
that thy divine art, as thou callest thy twanging
upon the harp, and soiling slips of parchment, had
taught thee that those who love share the cares
of each other. It cuts our mistress to the very
heart to hear the King speak against the Primate; and last night she spoke the saddest
things you ever heard, and she would not eat
her evening meal, but went hanging her sweet
head a one side, and talked of dying,—of the
world being a blank without a friend. She
called it a living grave, and made many other
doleful comparisons. But I should not care,"
added she, dashing the tear from her eye, "how
much they made me sad, if I could but lessen
her own sorrows."

"Bless thee, my dear Maud, for thy kind feeling," exclaimed the minstrel, pressing her to his bosom, "I will never call my life my own while she doth need it; thou shalt see that I will make amends for my past negligence, and ———"

What he intended to have said was cut short by the sudden appearance of Gamas Gobbo, who rushed up with his wing-like arms, waving with a double-quick motion; and buzzing loud as the hum of an hundred bees, while the signs of distress were depicted upon his sallow parchment-looking countenance; and imitating the tramping of a horse with his feet, he made signs for them to speed in the direction of Oxford.

"The child is lost," exclaimed Maud, and uttering a loud shriek, she rushed into the thicket. But Pierre de Vidal, who understood the signs of the idiot, instantly followed in the direction which he took, and both set off like race-horses; Gamas, however, leading the way

before the minstrel many a long yard, and
showing no more signs of fatigue than a black-
bird startled from her nest.

To account for the sudden absence of the
young prince, (for such we must suppose him to
be by birth,) we must return to the commence-
ment of the present chapter. The rushing
sound in the underwood, which the light ear of
the minstrel readily detected, and which Maud
innocently attributed to the startled stag that
the hardy boy had aroused, was occasioned by
none other than Oliphant Ugglethred, who
stumbled while attempting to secret himself
behind a clump of hazels. He had long before
been prowling in the neighbourhood of the park,
and had more than once discovered Pierre de
Vidal and Maud together in the same shady
haunts; but no sooner did he become acquainted
with the quality of the child, than he determined
at once upon seizing him. To effect this more
securely and prevent any sudden alarm, he
glided along with the stealthy pace of an Indian

from covert to covert, still keeping behind the
boy, until, having found a favourable shelter of
fern and hazels, he ventured beyond him, then
shot off through the underwood, by which he
was concealed. The fearless child, fancying
that he had again come upon the haunt of the
stag, followed the rustling sound at full speed,
hallooing at the top of his voice, and regardless
of the thorns and brambles, which pierced his
hard and naked legs. Onward did Oliphant
Ugglethred still allure him, in the direction
where his horse was hidden, for he had provided
himself with a high-mettled steed in case of
danger; but just as he thought he might safely
venture upon his unsuspecting victim, Gamas
Gobbo made his appearance, and he was as
familiar with the winding of every wood and
path in the vast chase, as the hart that had
been thrice hunted ; Gamas buzzed aloud, and
attempted to withdraw his little charge from the
thicket, for it was nothing unusual for the boy
to wander away for hours together under the

guidance of Gobbo; but on this occasion the
high-spirited little fellow refused to obey, and
aimed one of his headless shafts at the idiot, as
a sign of his rebellion. To this Gamas was
soon reconciled, and as several bees were humming and alighting upon the wild woodbines,
which made the very air in that part of the wood
redolent of their perfume; he was so busied
in his favourite amusement, and had bounded
to such a distance, that he was speedily out of
sight of the child. This was the favourable
moment for the ruffian, who springing up in an
instant, exclaimed. "The stag! the stag! I
have shot him with my cross-bow;" and
seizing the child by the hand, who was eager
enough to follow him, he half-dragged and half-
led him to where his steed stood secured to the
stem of an oak. While Ugglethred was busied
in unloosing the bridle, the boy, now suspecting
that all was not right, attempted to escape; but
he had not retreated many yards, before the
ruffian had thrown himself into the saddle, and

pursuing him, he made a stoop like an hawk, and with one jerk of his powerful arm, he was placed before him; and in another instant the hoofs of his steed were heard ringing through the wood, with a sound like distant thunder. The idiot, who had missed his companion, just came up in time to see him borne away, and having buzzed and shook his fist, and followed them a considerable distance, until they were out of sight; he retreated, as our readers are aware, to apprize Maud and the minstrel of the disaster.

CHAPTER VIII.

Ah, that deceit should steal such gentle shapes,
And with a virtuous visor hide deep vice!

Most smiling, smooth, detested parasites,
Courteous destroyers, affable wolves, meek bears,
You fools of fortune, trencher friends, time's flies,
Cap and knee slaves, vapours, and minute jacks.
                                        SHAKSPEARE.

LIKE a performer in a fair, who amuses the
crowd, by showing his dexterity in throwing up
and catching the various gilt balls which he
produces; so are we compelled to work our
chapters by different shiftings and crossings,
and jerkings, now before, then again behind,
laying down and taking up, yet constantly
keeping one or another in motion, until the last
solitary ball falls, is caught, and the crowd dis-
perses.   Some (like our readers,) who are
passing by, look on and exclaim, " It is an old

trick," without waiting to see the whole number in play, their tastes leading them further on to where another is exhibiting his dancing-bear, or monkey, which can play a thousand antics. Others regard not the particular sights, but jostle on through the crowd, only anxious to walk through the fair, without pausing at any one place, just to say that they have been there, and venturing their opinions upon what they have not seen, and consequently know but little. A few there are who like the performance to pass on quickly, and be soon over; considering every pause that depicts the passions a waste of time; such would wish to see a play of Shakspeare's represented in less time than they can read it in their closets. But authors, like actors, take their own time, and the audience must "sit out the play," or retire; they having the privilege still left them to grumble, and not come again.

Leaving, then, Oliphant Ugglethred to pursue

his course through the most intricate paths of the park of Woodstock, we must again convey our readers to the ancient palace of Oxford, where Queen Eleanor still continued to reside, surrounded by her companions of evil, and seeking to abet every plan which militated against her royal husband. The quarrel between Henry and Becket, had just fallen out as she wished it; and as the flax was already ignited, she now set about bringing it to a flame, that it might be the more readily consumed. Beside fomenting the feud between the monarch and the primate, and laying down plans for the destruction of Rosamond, whom she hated the more that Henry absented himself from her, she had also contrived to sow dissension in the distant realms of Poictou, and it was more than probable that the presence of the king himself would be required to quell them. Laymen and Churchmen, and Norman nobles in armour, were constantly passing to and from Oxford to

Woodstock; and during their calls at the former place, it was nothing uncommon for Eleanor to waylay such as had before been sounded, and to win them over to her own interests. We have before stated that her figure was commanding in the highest degree, and that her features possessed a beauty well adapted for admiration in that barbarous age; and well did she know how to make use of these powers, for there were very few of the haughty Norman barons, whose ungauntleted hands she had retained within the chisseled marble of her own, or into whose countenances she had darted the deep lustre of her own dark eyes, but what went away with some such expression as " Holy Virgin ! what power this Queen hath over us." " Who could look into her face and deny her aught ?" " She would make a priest forget his prayers;" or, " No marvel that she captivated the Saracen; by the mass ! her eyes hath shot through my armour, hauberk, and plate."

These, be it remarked, like the shepherd in Esop, had only gazed upon the sea when it was calm; they had not beheld those antics of pretty devilry which it was so much more natural for her to play off; nor had they a notion, that under so honied a surface, was concealed so much bitter wormwood and gall. The news of the mighty change which had taken place between the king and primate flew like wild-fire, and numbers who were ignorant of Eleanor's share in the matter, were, at the time when we again undraw the curtain, met in the hall of Oxford to condole with her.

Whatever Eleanor did, be it remembered, was always made to appear as if undertaken only for the glory of Henry; and many, w could see no deeper than the surface, enlisted into her plots, with a firm belief that they should be serving their monarch the better, the more that they did her bidding. There

were a few cunning foxes, however, who
listened with a suspicious glance, tapped
their mailed heels upon the floor of the hall,
hummed and ha'ed, and screwed together their
lips, pulled their chain gauntlets on and off, and
writhed their arms about as if the vent-brace
caused them pain. Some of these were men
who had seen the court of Louis of France, or
joined in the Crusade, and knew more of
Eleanor's real character, than she herself
supposed. These were men, to use an apt
but common phrase, who " were not to be bit."

Without pausing to dwell much upon any
particular character, saving the queen herself,
(for such we must call her, in spite of the
injustice done to Rosamond,) we shall at once
scribe the scene as it appeared on the day
following the quarrel, presuming that our
readers are aware that all similar scenes of
condolence are mere form, and just mean as
much as the calls made upon one another in the

fashionable world in the present day, after some
splendid ball — namely nothing ; unless some
patron-hunter has his eye on a particular point of
interest ; then his hopes and wishes and fears
multiply accordingly.

On a huge, unwieldy, and richly-carved
oaken chair on the dais, was seated Queen
Eleanor, endeavouring to look as dejected as
a sick woman, and speaking in an affected
and lower tone of voice than was her usual
custom, as if she had more cause to mourn
the quarrel between Henry and his favourite,
than any other ; but the unusual brightness of
her eyes sometimes gave the lie to her action
and speech ; for there the devil reigned in his
own fiery and natural form. Every now and
then, when she seemed to be the least observed,
her dark eye-brows were suddenly contracted,
and would have met, but for the angry furrow
which wrinkled her forehead : then again they
as suddenly relaxed, and fell with an apparent

gentleness upon the first countenance that approached : then again they were quickly cast down, and the same deep furrow darkened that otherwise smooth and beautiful brow.

"The Lord hath wrought in his own due time," said a Norman abbot, who had before been in converse with Eleanor. "I told your highness that this sudden conversion boded no good to our sovereign lord the king, but dared not to dream of his ingratitude. But whenever did a Saxon miss a chance to bite the hand that fed him ?"

"It is that which I fear the most," replied this pretty piece of iniquity, throwing an apparent pity into her countenance, which her firm-set lips gave the lie to. "You know not, my Lord Abbot, how this sudden quarrel hath unhinged me ; and the more do I feel it by reflecting that I, too, was instrumental in placing the Archbishop so high in his Highness's favour. But, assuredly this slight wound may yet be healed. The Primate will humble himself, and confess that he hath done wrong, and the King will again regain his wonted composure, and there will be no further innovation made against his power,—a power which I would fain see upheld, if it can be done without further severing their good will to each other."

" Your Highness is ever willing to be a peace-maker," said another bulky prelate, bowing low, with a most finished and court-like smile, which was faintly returned by the Queen; although no one present better knew the character of Eleanor than himself. " But surely, to rebel against the commands of our Sovereign Lord, is to rebel against Heaven itself; seeing that it is by the grace of Heaven that the King ruleth. And it is written,—hem!—hem!— *gravy* — no — *gravis ira regum semper*, — which none knoweth better than the worthy Primate himself; therefore, as one in our own day hath it, ' He who thrusteth his hand into the lion's mouth, must expect to feel his teeth.' But this comes from *obscuris ortus parentibus*; which your Highness knows well, signifieth — but— *me fugit memoria*;—I will give you the meaning at another time."

" Hath no one been made acquainted with the measures which his Grace intendeth to pursue, to bring back our beloved Primate to his allegiance ?" enquired Eleanor, with a look of apparent indifference. But she had scarcely asked the question, before Gilbert Foliot entered, his face red with rage, and raising his voice so that all around might hear him, he exclaimed, " The King hath come to a determination that the clergy shall no longer be tried before an ecclesiastical court for their crimes ; but like common felons, be in future subject to the criminal tribunal. He spoke it in mine own hearing ; and swore by his deepest oath, that he would not rest until it were done, and bade me to make it known forthwith."

Like masses of dark and distorted clouds, which are seen journeying over the face of heaven during a storm, and all making to that part of the sky which looks like an island of blackness; so did every monk, abbot, and bishop, and all who were connected with the church, move instantaneously to the lower end of the hall, where the greater part of the clergy were assembled.

Many a glance of sly mockery and silent triumph might be traced in the countenances of the Norman nobles whom they passed; and as Queen Eleanor received a whisper from an attendant to withdraw, she could scarcely refrain from laughing outright. Nor could she even then keep silence as she passed the abbot, who had so readily taken the part of Henry against Becket. But with one of those peculiar arch looks, such as a handsome woman only can assume, she said, " I trust your reverence will instil into the minds

of your holy brethren, those lessons of obedience
which you yourself have so well digested ; that
to rebel against the commands of the King, is
to rebel against Heaven." The holy father
wished at heart that her Highness was with
Sathanus ; and showing his teeth at a mail-clad
baron who burst out into a loud fit of laughter,
he hutched up his cord,—gave his cowl a twist,
and hurried among the dark conclave at the
further end of the hall.

" The King hath declared war against
Heaven," said a bishop, who looked more like
a representative of Bacchus than the church ;
" hath invaded the Holy Temple ! and attacked
the sacred privileges of Christ !"

" Hath struck at the root of our private
flagellations, and penitential severities," said
another, who was so fat that he could scarcely
see out of his sleepy eyes. " Who will undergo
abstinence, and all that rigorous discipline
which, for the love of Heaven, we inflict upon

ourselves, if we are to be punished by the hands of godless men?"

"Or who that has seen a holy back scourged by the common thong used in the Hundred?" said a third; "or heard a priest cry for mercy like a felon, will believe that we can absolve, and grant forgiveness to others? or come to confession, when our own misdeeds are bruited abroad by the rabble?"

"Let us hope," said a fourth, "that the Primate at our head will not forsake us, for the sake of the few who have fallen from him."

"Hope makes a poor loaf," said another irreligious rascal; "and prayer a worse pasty; we must show a bold front, brethren. Cannot the King ruffle one feather of the fowl, without pulling at the whole body? We must shun the stag that he is hunting, and when it would harbour amongst us, butt him away again, with our heads. Better that the wolf carry away the shepherd, than every sheep in the fold."

Leaving the conclave in the midst of their clamour and argument, which increased like the cackling of a score of hens all driven from their nests; we shall follow Eleanor into another apartment, whither she had been summoned by Oliphant Ugglethred. When the Queen opened the door, she was startled by the presence of the child, whose passion was now moderated, and was imploring the villain to take him back again to his mother.

"Who hast thou here?" said Eleanor, her eyes glancing at first affectionately over the handsome features of the boy.

"The urchin will be ready enough to answer your Highness," said Ugglethred, with his usual effrontery; "and you have heard both the name of his father and mother before."

"Come," said she, putting out her hand, and burying her taper fingers among the clustering curls of the child's hair, and speaking with a kindness which was for the moment natural, "tell me the name of thy father, then I may know where thy mother dwelleth?"

"King Henry is my father," said the boy, unconscious of the presence he stood in; "and my mother's name is Rosamond; and this man stole me away from Maud; but my father will come soon."

"Why brought ye the bastard hither?" said the Queen, springing back, as if she had unconsciously touched a serpent; while her brow became suddenly dark, and her eyes seemed to blaze again upon Ugglethred, for she was satisfied at a glance that the features of the boy resembled Henry's.

"I could not find the lioness, so I brought the cub," replied the villain, without moving a muscle of his iron features.

"Couldst thou not have stabbed him in the lair?" inquired the Queen, not a shade of pity passing over her fine but fearful countenance, "without bringing him hither to tempt me to become his butcher?"

"I might have done as much," replied Ugglethred, "had I known that such had been your pleasure, although, to say truth, I care not to wet my dagger in the blood of a child, since such is the work of tender mothers and kind nurses."

The boy, meantime, had remained silent, and although he cast his piercing eyes from one to the other, yet was he not fully able to comprehend all that was passing; for in Ugglethred's countenance no sign of anger could be traced; and although the Queen from time to time cast an ominous glance upon him, yet he was scarcely conscious of the danger.

"Take him hence and dispatch him," said Eleanor, her cold cruel features undergoing no change. "You ought not to have brought the bastard into my presence."

" By your Highness's leave," said the ruffian, in the same careless tone as he would have addressed one of his equals; " I would first suggest that you endeavour to find out where his mother dwelleth, for as yet I have not been able to discover the hare on her seat, although I have kept careful watch."

" Couldst thou not play the interrogator?" said Eleanor, casting a scornful glance at Ugglethred : " I have heard thee boast that thou hadst means to cut short long arguments, and extract secrets; why dost thou leave thy work half finished ?"

" Thou art hard to please," replied the undaunted ruffian. " I have seen the day when thou wouldst have given me thanks for a smaller service than this; and methinks it would disgrace my calling, (villain though I own myself to be in your highness's most respected service,) were I to enforce my hard arguments, when a dip in the honey-pot, or a half-ripened apple, might wring from the urchin all you would obtain. I will do your bidding so far as it runneth with my humour;—but I will not kill this boy."

"No! no! you will not hurt me," said the child, stepping up to Ugglethred, and seizing the skirt of his tunic, for he now began to comprehend the danger, and felt alarmed at the savage looks of the Queen; for her countenance was deadly pale with anger, and her lips quivered again with savage vengeance, as she cast a withering and baleful glance at Ugglethred, as if she would annihilate him by her looks.

"Villain!" exclaimed she, springing forward like an enraged tigress, and seizing the boy by the hair, while she drew forth a dagger which was concealed in her belt, and brandished it over the head of the child, whose loud screams now rung through the apartment:—"Villain!

I will be revenged on thee; nor shall the prey now escape my hands !"

" Do as you list," said Ugglethred, without interfering, " I shed blood as I drink the juice of the grape, leaving that which is not fully ripe, to the fancy of those who like it."

The dagger was uplifted, and the bright blade glittered for a moment, as it caught the rays of light, ere it descended upon its victim, when the sound of a trumpet was heard without, and rang through every room of the palace. Eleanor paused a moment, with her fingers twined amid the clustering ringlets of the child's hair, whose loud cries now increased ; and as she stood with her large eyes dilated, and her bosom heaving beneath its weight of passion, like a mountain struggling before an eruption, she bore no bad resemblance to some savage and Heathen priestess, wrought up to the highest pitch of brutal enthusiasm, and about to offer up a human sacrifice to her idol. But ere the blow was dealt, the door was thrown open with a force that made the huge posts to shake again, and King Henry rushing into the apartment, wrenched the dagger from the hand of Eleanor, and struck her a blow which left her senseless on the floor of the apartment. Ugglethred escaped,—and the child was borne safely to Rosamond: whose grief for his absence we leave to the imagination of our readers.

CHAPTER IX.

Muse not that I thus suddenly proceed ·
For what I will, I will, and there's an eud.

Let them pronounce the steep Tarpeian death.
Vagabond, exile, flaying.   Pent to linger
But with a grain a day, I would not buy
Their mercy at the price of one fair word.
SHAKSPEARE.

TIME, in the pages of a romance, is like distance to the Eastern genii : ere we have spoken
it is past, and we again take up our characters
and pursue our story, as if we had never once
halted, or affairs had undergone no change
since we parted.   The quarrel between Henry
and the Primate had daily grown more serious,
and the former had made several attempts to
overthrow the independence of the church, to
break up its ecclesiastical courts, and, as was
before stated, subject the clergy to the common

tribunals. This Becket steadily resisted; sometimes appearing to yield, when the threats of the monarch grew dangerous, then again presenting himself in open defiance, and daring Henry to do his worst. We pass by the meeting at Westminster, and all the annoyances to which the primate subjected himself, rather than yield up the independence of the church. Neither shall we bring before our readers the hotly disputed contest at Clarendon, when Becket, threatened by an armed force, promised to sign the articles; and after a long penance, withdrew his pledge. All these are matters of history, and are familiar to those who are at all acquainted with the annals of our country, and would only occupy the pages of our story with information which may be found in numerous other works. To such of our readers who wish to be fully acquainted with these events, we would recommend the perusal of Sharon Turner's impartial " History of Egland during

the Middle Ages," "Rapin's England," "Lyttle-
ton's History of Henry the Second," or, "Mr.
Berrington's defence of Becket;" the latter
taking the most favourable view of the Archbishop's conduct, and in our humble opinion,
placing it in too lenient a light. But it is not
in a work of fiction like ours, (built upon the
mere skeleton of historical truth,) that we can
enter into a discussion of these subjects; we
write to amuse, and not enlighten; to please
rather than instruct; and only profess to keep
within the probable boundary of truth where it
best suits our purpose. Leaving then all these
matters behind, we shall again commence our
story, on the morning of the last day of trial
at Northampton, where, as Sharon Turner says,
"Henry had summoned a parliament obviously
to crush the now hated Becket." When all
the nobles and bishops had fallen from him,
and when an inferior spirit would have humbled
himself in the dust,—when stripped of all his

honours, and retaining only the primacy, without the power of acting up to its dignities, and
after having stood a trial which lasted three
days, and during which the king brought all
the charges against him that malice could in-
vent, or meanness devise, (many of them trivial
and vexatious and unworthy of a hearing,)
Becket rose himself again ; the spirit of the
soldier, and the high soul of the churchman
once more blazed out, for he felt humbled at
the concessions which he had already made,
and which were all despised or rejected ; Henry
being determined that he should no longer
remain Primate of England.

But Becket was not the man to be subdued
by threats, and when all his enemies thought
that he was humbled, and would resign his
power at the feet of the King, then he arose
like a brave knight who has but been stunned in
the combat, and awakens to the renewed charge
armed with double courage, ashamed that

he has lain so long idle in the lists. Urged to submit by the Pope, besieged by the trembling bishops, and threatened by the savage barons, he still resisted their combined powers, and boldly pursued his own course; and after the fatigue and terror of three days' trial, we again bring him before our readers, supposing that a long time had elapsed since the first outbreak of the quarrel at Woodstock.

The dull autumnal morning that broke in upon the apartment where Becket slumbered, seemed to harmonise with the approaching struggle. Sometimes a sunbeam beat its way through the masses of cloud, then was again suddenly dimmed,—leaving it doubtful whether gloom or brightness would prevail. The faithful attendant, Gryme, had sprung from the pallet at the foot of his master's bed, and while he hung for a moment over his pillow, ere he ventured to awaken him, the same thoughts which we have attempted to convey to the reader, passed through his mind. There was a deep but silent agony depicted on the features of the Archbishop; and while his hands clutched the embroidered coverlet, he appeared like one who had closed his eyes, and made up his thoughts to die sternly. Low murmurs also escaped his lips for a moment or two,—muttered rapidly, as if giving vent to a torrent of passion, then again stealing forth slowly and feebly, like one who pleads humbly, or is in prayer; their purport was, however, inaudible. While his face rested in half-shadow, he gradually relaxed his grasp from the rich covering; and as he unconsciously threw out his arm, the drapery was removed from his broad chest, and revealed the rough shirt of hair, which he constantly wore under his splendid garments in voluntary penance.

Once did his stern features unbend, just as a stray sunbeam shot through the stained lattice; it was but for a moment, and the cloud

again gathered upon his brow, as the overhanging gloom fell upon the chamber. The attendant stood by, and calmly watched shade after
shade pass in silence over the features of the
restless sleeper; not daring, however, to awaken
him, until the frown was cleared from the ample
brow, well knowing that it was dangerous to
arouse the lion while slumbering in such a
mood.

At length the Primate awoke, and passing
his hand over his eyes, as if uncertain of the
situation he occupied, his glance alighted upon
Gryme; and he inquired if the monks had yet
assembled in the chapel.

"Thou forgettest, holy father," replied the
attendant, "that we are far from the choir of
Canterbury, and that this is the final day of
trial, when thou must again face thine enemies,
and either triumph or fall before them."

"True! true! answered the Archbishop in a
melancholy tone. "And yet I stood before

them even now," muttered he to himself, "and felt the hands of the bishops tugging at the cross, as if they would wrench it from my grasp. But they shall this day know with whom they have to deal," added he, springing from the couch, and planting his naked foot upon the rugged bear-skin which was spread on the floor for he had only divested himself of his upper garments when he retired to rest.

For a moment or two he seemed to stand in utter unconsciousness of what was taking place, so entirely was he occupied with his own thoughts, and held out his arms almost mechanically, while Gryme put on the plain under-tunic which he commonly wore. Instantly, however, recollecting himself, he tore off the garment with such force as to rip it down the front, and casting it upon the floor, exclaimed, " Bring forth my robes of office, with the mitre and the silver cross. I will wear none of these."

The monk paused a moment, as if he expected the order to be retracted; for it was nothing uncommon for the haughty churchman to issue his mandates, and countermand them in a breath; but when the abrupt question was put of " Didst thou not hear me?" in rather an angry tone, he then fixed his gaze upon the Archbishop in astonishment, and said, " Assuredly thou meanest not to venture forth in the robes of thine holy office; consider, reverend father, that those who are against thee will not fail to interpret such a thing to thy disadvantage;—will, perchance, set down to pride, and recklessness of humility, what thou thyself doest as a duty."

" What trowest thou, that I will appear before that assembly again in aught that becometh not my dignity?" replied the prelate, a flush of anger fading over his features as he spoke. " Knowest thou not that they would be the first to exclaim, ' He hath humbled himself, and cometh forth to be rebuked?' No! by the holy order of which it hath pleased Heaven to make me the head, they shall, by the grace of God, this day see that I am not unworthy of being their leader." He paused short; for as he waved his arm aloof in the earnestness of his speech, the rough hair-shirt grazed his shoulder by the motion, and reminded him that his feelings but ill-accorded with the garment of penitence which he wore. " Leave me for a short space," added he, waving his hand for the attendant to depart, who, without replying, quitted the chamber.

Left alone,—with slow and measured step, and arms folded on his bosom, did Becket pace the apartment; while a thousand contending emotions rushed through his bosom, like the headlong waves struggling and foaming to overleap the narrow outlet which the torrent has torn through the river-banks. In vain did he attempt to quell these contending passions.

He took up his beads,—every drop of which was formed of the purest gold;—but ere he had numbered three; the whole string was gathered up in his unconscious grasp, and he was again pacing the apartment with long and furious strides; every step of which caused the richly painted window to chatter. The names of Henry, Hereford, and York, also fell from his lips; and when he made mention of Clarendon, and reverted to the deed which he promised to sign, he stood as suddenly still in the centre of the room, as if he had been struck by a thunderbolt; while the nails of his fingers doubled up into the palms of his hands with a fierce involuntary grasp, and his brow grew dark as midnight. At length he heaved a deep sigh, and passing his hand over his face, threw himself into a massy chair, and sat motionless as a statue.

The dark spot gradually left his brow, and the stern struggle seemed in some measure to

have abated ; but how the decision had ter-
minated, there were no traces left behind to tell.
A deep and settled purpose was, however,
visible; but whether it was the fearful tranquillity that reigns at intervals between the
outbursts of the tempest, or the sure and settled
calm, that compressed lip and thoughtful brow
told not.

He arose, and stepping up to where a rich
crucifix was erected against the wall, threw
himself down before it, and with bowed head
and folded hands, remained for a few moments
kneeling in deep and fervent prayer. This
over, he bathed his face and hands in a silver
ewer, and having finished his ablutions, again
summoned his attendant into the apartment.

Gryme entered, bearing in his hand a loaf of
the coarsest bread, and having placed it on
the table, returned again with a cup of water,
and a golden bowl filled with cold green herbs,
which he placed beside the loaf. Coarse as

this food was, even beyond that eaten by the lowliest serf, the prelate partook of it with an apparent relish, and washed it down with a hearty draught from the silver cup, although the water was green and nauseous, through the sprigs of fennel which had purposely been immersed therein. But such was his constant meal, morning and evening, and he rarely partook of any other banquet: it was the diet that he subjected himself to on almost all ordinary occasions, and this, together with the severe penances which he occasionally underwent, did much to throw the charge of hypocrisy upon the shoulders of his accusers. Ambitious he was, to a height that perhaps became not a churchman; but even his greatest enemies must admit that he never lost sight of the holy cause which he advocated, or sought to barter his trust for his personal aggrandisement. He was one of those spirits which were born to lead, or perish, and was determined to

sway the pastoral crook over the church as un-
interruptedly as King Henry did his sceptre over
his English subjects.

Becket felt that he should only make himself despised by further humiliation; that he
had already yielded too much to Henry; nay
further, that he had sank in his own estimation,
and his proud soul kindled up again, while
these thoughts passed through his mind.

"Hath Mortenel or Anselm inquired after
mine health this morning?" said Becket.

"No one has been here as yet," answered
Gryme. "I marvel that none of the bishops
have called; they were wont to attend us
earlier."

"I marvel not at these things," replied the
Prelate. "Gryme! they are falling from me.
The cowardly herd!" continued he, pushing
back the coarse food; "while they deemed
me secure in the king's favour, while my table
and my wealth satisfied all their wants, and

while I fed them and their retainers by hundreds daily, the base sycophants were ready to lick the dust from my feet. But now, when they think that I have fallen from my high estate, that my coffers are exhausted, and my power on the wane, they would leave me to fight the battle alone ; nay, be the very foremost to plant their feet upon my neck when I have fallen. I, who would make them what they ought to be, and break asunder the fetters by which they are bound down."

"Arm thyself with patience, holy father," said Gryme, who never neglected to check the proud archbishop when he saw him thus yielding to his fierce passions : "remember that the holy Saviour himself suffered for the good of the church."

" Patience !" echoed Becket, with a contemptuous look :—" And thinkest thou that patience would be a virtue in this cause ? I tell thee that I have more need of anger; that the struggle is not to be decided by patience and words; but more after the manner of a brave knight, battling against odds, who has more than mortal anger in his breast, and more than human valour in his arm, and whose forbearance might well be called cowardice."

"Thou speakest but too true, holy father," answered Gryme, " if thy quarrel is in behalf of heaven and the church."

" The quarrel is Heaven's," replied Becket in a tone that but ill accorded with one who was at the head of the Church of Peace, " and in Heaven's cause have I buckled this armour on my back, and borne even the wrath of the king without blenching. Nor will I set him an evil example, by resigning the sceptre which I sway over the church, lest, when he is hard bestead, he might in an ill hour give up his crown. The Pope made me what I am, and by him only will I be deposed. No! should every cowardly priest fall from my side, alone I will maintain this quarrel."

" Nor will I fall from thee," said the faithful monk, "an' thou remainest but true to thyself. I will take up my cross and follow thee through all evil report."

" I know thee to be faithful," said the Archbishop, extending his hand to Gryme; "and thou shalt not say that thou wert servant to one who dared not to maintain his own dignity. This day shalt thou behold me keeping all my foes at bay, and if I conquer them not, thou shalt see me retreat with honour, like a hart to the covert, in the very teeth of the hounds that are baying me."

Saying which, he began to robe himself, and by the assistance of Gryme, in readiness for the approaching and decisive struggle.

Meantime a vast crowd were assembled without, all waiting anxiously for the appearance

of the Archbishop; for as the higher orders
fell from him, and his danger became more apparent, so did he, on the other hand advance in
the favour of the lower classes,—who from time
to time rent the air, with loud shouts of " Long
live the Archbishop of Canterbury!" " Down
with the Norman Bishops!" " Long life to the
bold Saxon!" But when the gate of the court-
yard was thrown open, and the proud Prelate
himself appeared, mounted on a superb charger,
and bearing the silver crucifix in his hand, the
shouts became deafening, and even reached to
the hall of trial where Henry was seated with
his nobles, and once caused the ruddy cheek of
the monarch to turn pale.

For several moments the Archbishop's course
was impeded by the dense numbers who flocked
around to crave his blessing, and while he held
the richly ornamented bridle in his left hand,
with the right he waved the silver crucifix over
their heads, and blessed them as he rode along.

And well did he wear his dignity on that eventful morning; for as his fine form rose high above the assembled crowd, and his rich dress mingled with the trappings of his steed; while his jewelled mitre blazed in the morning sun; they all seemed to draw a grace from that god-like figure, who with a calm brow and fearless heart moved along, looking as if he were born to decide the fate of empires.

Leaving Becket with the multitude, which kept increasing as they ascended the hilly street of Northampton, while numberless heads were thrust out of every little arched and ancient window to salute him as he passed; we will conduct our readers to the hall of the palace, where King Henry, surrounded by all his court, awaited the Archbishop's approach. Occupying the highest seat at the farthest end of the hall, sat the monarch himself, overlooking the whole scene; while the tables, which were arranged in the form of a T, and were covered with

various documents, all relating to the trial of
Becket, were stretched out before him. On
the right hand of King Henry sat the grave
Glanvil,—whom we have before introduced to
our readers as the greatest judge and law-maker
of that age,—his shaggy brows were bent upon
a large sheet of parchment,—the contents of
which absorbed his whole thoughts. To the
left of the monarch was seated the Earl of
Leicester, in deep conversation with two bishops,
whose outstretched necks and bald heads,—
which ever and anon they nodded, as they assumed looks of great wisdom, bore no inapt
resemblance to Chinese mandarins. Henry
seemed ill at ease in his seat; then he fixed his
large blue eyes upon one or another around
him, as if he would fain read their thoughts;
and as the shouts of the multitude drew nearer,
he passed his hand before his brow, and at last
remained absorbed in deep meditation. Towards the door stood a group of bishops, among

whom the figures of York and Hereford were conspicuous; they were in deep conversation, and kept glancing from time to time at the King.

Along the sides of the hall stood numbers of the Norman barons, some sheathed in mail, and grasping their various weapons,—some with their visors up—with the butt-end of their long lances resting on the floor, gazed carelessly on the scene around them; others were leaning on their heavy cross-handled swords, and either conversing with each other in low tones, or buried in their own contemplations. A few rested against the pillars of the hall, and seemed motionless as statues; while their armour flashed back the flood of light which shot down from the high windows, or wore a deep, solemn, and bronzy hue, as they stood in the shadow of the columns. Even the grim and carved figures which held shields in their hands, and looked down from the richly ornamented roof, seemed somehow to belong to the scene, as if their hideous wooden faces took an interest in the proceedings that were going on below. One of the images in especial had arrested the eye of an old baron, who kept constantly shifting his glance from the figure to Glanvil, as if he sought to trace a resemblance between it and the judge.

At length the shouts of the mob announced the near approach of the Archbishop, and echoed along the vaulted roof of the hall, so loud as even to draw the glance of Glanvil from the parchment, and cause his deep and sunken grey eyes to look towards the door. King Henry also awoke from his reverie, and looked fixedly in the same direction; while the quick quivering of his lips told that, in spite of his affected calmness, he was deeply excited.

Without the hall door, stood the Archbishop of York, together with Gilbert Foliot, the

Bishop of Hereford, and Hilary of Chichester;
and great was the astonishment of these divines
when they beheld the undaunted prelate approaching in all the panoply of spiritual defiance. They gazed upon each other in mute
astonishment; for they expected that Becket
would that day appear in the most humble
guise, not doubting even that he would approach
bare-footed, and throw himself at the King's
feet, to sue for forgiveness. Nay, their wishes
even carried them further; for they anticipated
seeing him spurned by Henry; stripped of all
his power, and placed in one of the lowest sta-
tions in the church. But when, in place of this,
they beheld him approach in all his power,
armed as it were with the thunder of the church,
and springing up with all that courage which
was so natural to his character, and which at
once declared that he now stood in full and
open defiance before the King, they were as
much startled as if a volcano had opened at

their feet. They stood with uplifted hands and mouths agape, while their eyes remained as fixed in astonishment, as if an apparition had sprung up before them.

The Bishop of Hereford was the first to speak, and approaching him with an affected humility, he seized on the silver crucifix with both hands and said, " Permit me, holy father, to bear the sacred emblem of our salvation before thee. It ill becometh thee to carry that which it is the office of a suffragan to bear."

" Back, hypocrite !" said Becket, " art thou not ashamed to stand before me ? Back, I say, or here upon this very threshold, and in the face of this multitude, I will publish thy shame."

The Bishop shrank back like a dog before his angry master, and Hilary of Chichester, with a low bow, offered himself as cross-bearer, and even dared to take hold of the holy symbol.

The Archbishop looked upon him with a

glance of withering hatred, and by a powerful effort wrenched the cross from his grasp, while he exclaimed, with a look of triumph, that caused his fine eyes to kindle,—" I know thy kindness, but it is most meet that this day I should bear the cross myself. Under the defence of this holy emblem I am safe, it is the ensign of heaven, and denotes under what prince I serve."

The Bishop gnashed his teeth with rage, to see himself thus foiled, both by the superior strength, and deeper laid policy of Becket. The Archbishop of York was also pale with fear, and anger ; and while his bloodless lips quivered, and his whole frame trembled from head to foot, he said, " Proud Prelate, thou art defying our lord the King, to enter his court in this guise. But remember, he hath a sword, the point of which is sharper than thy pastoral staff."

" Ah ! darest thou to threaten me, base sycophant ?" replied Becket, turning upon the trembling Archbishop like an enraged tiger, and brandishing the heavy cross over his head. "An' thou keepest not thy tongue in greater reverence, I will pour forth the curses of the holy church upon thee, and excommunicate thee beyond the pale of salvation. As for thee," added he, glancing upon the Bishop of Chichester, "I marvel that thou darest to show thy face in this assembly, when but a month agone one of thy nearest relations was hung for a thief and a robber." Saying which he strode into the hall, with the stately step of a conqueror; and more like one who was about to sit in judgment amid the assembly, than stand before them on trial.

The three prelates followed in the rear, with malicious and downcast looks, like cowed dogs whose inclinations would lead them to bite; but having met with so bold a rebuff, are compelled to confine their wrath within the compass of a few subdued growls.

With his silver cross elevated,—his stately form erect, and his countenance still bearing traces of the late explosion of his wrath, while his rich mantle swept its ample folds along the floor, and a few of his most faithful attendants following in due order,—the high-souled prelate trod with a firm foot up the centre of the hall; while baron and bishop gave way before him, like waves that yield to the prow of some stately vessel which steps with crowded canvass over the bosom of the deep.

As yet King Henry was not aware of his presence; for he still sat with his elbow resting upon the arm of the huge oaken chair which he occupied, while his brow was half-buried in the palm of his hand; and so deeply was he absorbed in his own thoughts, that he was un-

conscious of what was taking place before him.
But when a low deep murmur ran through the
hall, like the groaning sound which sweeps
through the forest, as if to announce the coming
storm; he passed his hand over his brow, and
sitting upright on his seat, his eyes met the
collected and angry glance of Thomas à
Becket.

The monarch leant forward in his seat, as if
to assure himself that it was not a vision which
had sprung up before him. But when he
became satisfied that the daring figure was the
Archbishop of Canterbury, whose steadfast eye
fell upon him unmoved, while he held up the
silver cross, which, like an ægis, appalled all
who looked upon it, the dark lines instantly
gathered upon his brow,—his teeth became
clenched,—his hands doubled up with a kind
of convulsive grasp,—and while his bright eyes
seemed to shoot forth fire, his whole face be-

came a deep crimson, like a fiery sunset
sinking amid the gathering storm. All eyes
were fixed upon the King and Becket; but not
a lip moved,—not a sound was heard through-
out the vast hall;—men seemed to hold their
breath while they watched the upheaving of
the tempest; as if they expected that its first
burst would bring the whole roof about their
heads. The followers of Becket trembled; but
the Prelate neither moved eye nor lip, nor was
there a shadow of fear upon his countenance;
and while he stood in dignified silence, he
seemed to fill the body of the hall; for the eye
sought in vain to rest upon aught saving his
godlike figure and the silver cross which he
held on high: even the vacant space which
they had left around him, pointed him out as
the only mark worthy of the tempest's wrath;
for he stood like a gigantic oak in the midst of
a vast plain overlooking the dwarf trees around

him, and stretching his topmost boughs towards the black and angry heavens.

The first sign of the king's exploding wrath was to clutch the hilt of the dagger in his belt, as if he was about to spring forward, and at one blow strike the haughty Churchman dead at his feet; but then his eye fell upon the cross, and springing from his seat like a tiger from the covert, he overturned the grave Glanvill in his rage, as he arose and exclaimed * " By God's eyes! I will have vengeance! he hath armed himself against me," saying which he rushed into an inner apartment, for, in the midst of his rage, he saw the impossibility of gratifying his vengeance on the spot, without calling down all the thunders of Christendom upon his head.

Like masses of clouds scattered over the face of heaven, and following in the rear of the

* This was Henry's usual oath when deeply enraged; and, according to the old chroniclers, the very words he uttered on this occasion. The whole of the following dialogue in this chapter is but a mere transcript from history.

tempest, so did the bishops and barons close upon the wake of the king, and enter the inner apartment, leaving Becket in the hall, accompanied only by a few of his own followers, and the lower clergy of the Church, who, unlike the rest of the high-fed and place-seeking dignitaries, boldly stood by the side of the Archbishop. Many of them were, however, pale with fear, and dreaded that the wrath of Henry would vent itself against the Primate, ere he departed. Not so with Becket: he stept up calmly to the side of the vast hall, and seated himself on a bench, and still holding the silver cross in his hands, he seemed to await his fate like a brave captain, who, when the decks are deserted, sits alone listening to the shrill wind, with rudder in hand, prepared to meet the first fierce outbreak of the storm, from which he is aware there is no retreating.

The faithful Gryme stood boldly beside his

master; neither of them, however, exchanging a word, so much was each engaged with his own thoughts. Once, however, they exchanged glances with each other, and that was at a moment when the uplifted voice of King Henry was heard from the inner apartment, sounding like distant thunder. Suddenly it ceased : then a sound as of many voices were heard in confusion together ; then the angry voice of Henry again broke forth, and overwhelmed them all.

At length the Bishop of Exeter rushed out of the inner apartment with a terrified countenance ; and, throwing himself at the feet of Becket, with an imploring look, said, " Have pity, holy father, upon thy brethren of the Church ; the King hath already struck down one of the Bishops who spoke in thy defence ; and hath sworn his most awful vow, that he will sheathe his dagger in the heart of the first who shall dare to excuse thy conduct. In pity,

lay aside the crucifix, and approach our sovereign lord with humility; conjure him by the
remembrance of your former friendship to overlook the past; if not for thyself, do it in compassion for the Church."

"Thou a servant of God—a pillar of His
Holy Church!" said Becket, with a concealed
sneer, " and fearest the anger of a king more
than the wrath of Heaven! Nay, flee, then;
for my part, I move not a step, until I have
maintained the dignity of mine high estate, and
stopped the mouths of these curs ! even in the
midst of their imagined triumph!"

Presently the whole of the bishops appeared
in a body, headed by Hilary of Chichester, who
thus spoke the sentiments of the deputation.
" Thou, Thomas à Becket, wast our Primate;
but now we thus publicly disavow thee, and
no longer acknowledge thee as the head of
our church. Thou hast broken thy oath, sworn·

to our sovereign lord, and we proclaim thee as a traitor, and a perjured Archbishop; nor will we any longer obey thy commands; but place ourselves and our cause in the hands of his Holiness the Pope, before whom we summon thee to answer."

" I hear what you say," replied Becket, without either arising from his seat or changing countenance; for he felt that the moment of triumph had not yet arrived. Stung with rage and covered with shame, the whole body again retreated into the inner apartment, like a mass of waters spurned back by the foot of the mighty rock, which their puny efforts could not wash a pebble from.

But the storm had not yet reached its height, and Becket calmly awaited further proofs of its fury. Nor had he to wait long before the whole of the barons and bishops came forth in a column, headed by Robert, Earl of Leicester, who held in his hand a parchment containing the sentence, which he proceeded to read in the usual form of the Norman court, and halting before Becket, began, " Oyez-ci! Oyez-ci!"

" Stop!" exclaimed the Archbishop, waving his hand as he arose, and drawing his form to its full height, while he planted his foot within an hand-breadth of the Earl's, and held the crucifix erect before him, as his eye glanced without blenching along the lines of his enemies. " Stop, son Earl! and hear me first. You are my children!—rebels although you be—nor have ye power to sit in judgment on your spiritual father. I forbid you, therefore, on pain of excommunication, to judge me. I deny the power of your tribunal; and leave my quarrel to the decision of the Pope, who alone on earth hath power over me. To him I now appeal; and having placed myself under the protection of the holy church and the apostolic see, I depart in peace."

A dead blank expression fell upon the faces of the whole assembly; they were caught in the very snare which they themselves had prepared. This counter-appeal came wholly unexpected;—their whole policy was overturned in a moment;—they stood baffled, confused, and beaten. Becket paused a moment ere he departed; turning upon them like a noble stag who shakes his antlers upon the yelping pack ere he betakes himself to the thicket,—then he trod with measured and stately step towards the door of the hall. When near the door, some of the courtiers' attendants hissed; and picking up straws and rushes, with which some parts of the hall were strewn, threw them at him, exclaiming, " Such a traitor and perjurer is not worthy to live !"

The spirit of the soldier was not yet, however, extinguished, for turning upon them with an angry countenance, and shaking the crucifix in their faces ; in a deep voice which caused the vaulted hall to ring again, he exclaimed, "Begone, base slaves, lest ye tempt me to smite you to the earth with this holy symbol. And you," added he, turning to the barons, who had called him traitor, "did not my holy calling forbid me, I would give back mine answer on the sword point to every coward of you who has dared to insult me."

The whole herd fell back, and a few there were who gave vent to their feelings in murmurs of applause, when they beheld the undaunted bearing of the high-souled Prelate. And many a bold eye that but an hour before had bent upon him in anger, now beamed with admiration at his valour, and vowed within themselves that they would follow so courageous a leader to the utmost ends of the earth.

At the hall door he again mounted his palfrey, and rode homeward in triumph, followed by the acclamations of the crowd, who rent the air with shouts, many exclaiming, " Blessed be God who hath delivered his faithful servant from the hands of his enemies.'' Deserted by nearly all the noble and powerful, the lower orders looked upon him as their champion, for he was almost the only Saxon who dared to stand up against the power of the King and barons, since the Norman conquest.

As he rode along, he bowed low, and blessed the crowd who saluted him, and returned his courtesy with thunders of acclaim. But a calm observer, who had looked narrowly into the fine countenance of the Prelate, would have seen that the smile with which he acknowledged the plaudits of the crowd, was accompanied by a troubled eye, and that on the least cessation of tumult, the lips became compressed and the brow furrowed. He was like some great actor on a stage, who, while he returns the greetings of his audience, has his mind wrapt up in the contemplation of the part he has yet to enact. He well knew the dangerous position in which he stood, for he had that day defied the King, and the whole power by which he was surrounded; nor was he ignorant that among the barons there were many desperate men, who neither regarded God nor the church, and would not, if occasion presented itself, hesitate a moment to take away his life. The Primate of England reached his residence amid the thunder of hundreds of voices, and bowing low as he alighted from his palfrey, entered the open gates with a smiling countenance, and a heavy heart.

CHAPTER X.

Are not these woods
More free from peril than the envious court?
Here feel we but the penalty of Adam,
The season's difference; as the icy fang,
And churlish chiding of the winter's wind;
Which, when it bites and blows upon my body,
Even till I shrink with cold, I smile, and say,—
This is no flattery: these are counsellors
That feelingly persuade me what I am.

As You Like It.

THE night which set in upon this memorable
day was rainy and dark, and the cold October
wind blew bleakly from the North, and swept
fiercely through the narrow and hilly streets
of Northampton. Stormy, however, as it was,
Becket well knew that no time must be lost,
for he had already received warning from a
faithful follower, that danger awaited him, and
was aware that there were those amongst his

enemies who would not hesitate to shed his blood. When the messenger also returned which he had despatched to King Henry, craving permission to leave England, with the answer that " he would think of it on the morrow," he was fully assured that measures would be put in force by the monarch to deprive him of his liberty, if he lingered in the town until that morrow came.

Such were the thoughts that passed through the Archbishop's mind, as he sat in the rude oaken chair, watching the faggots, as they crackled and blazed on the ample hearth, and filled the apartment with smoke, for it contained neither grate nor chimney.

Occasionally, however, the light of the ruddy flames fell upon his fine thoughtful countenance, or were flashed back again by the golden embroidery which decorated his rich canonical dress, for he had not yet doffed the garments

which he wore in the hall of trial. The silver
cross which he had also borne in his hand,
stood in the corner opposite to where he sat,
as if it had been cast aside like a bauble with
which a child was weary of playing. The rich
foot-cloth and the gaudy harness with which
his steed had that day been caparisoned, were
thrown together beside the mitre and cross,
and all were hidden or revealed, just as the
uncertain flames flashed, or darkened. Care
there was deeply imprinted on the brow of the
Archbishop, but such a collectedness was mingled therewithal, that he seemed like some
bold pilot, who, conscious that the wind and
waves are bearing him onward amid rocks and
quicksands, is determined never to quit the
helm, until the goodly vessel hath become a
wreck. He felt that he had upheld his course
in the very teeth of danger; and, if he could
no longer bear the brunt of the elements, he

could yet run into some inland creek, where the tempest might rave around him in vain.

He had not sat long alone before his faithful attendant Gryme entered the apartment, his garments drenched through with the rain.

" How lieth the land?" said Becket, raising his eyes to his follower as he spoke, and kicking the brands together to bring them to a flame; " are we already beleaguered, or is there yet time to begone?"

" Every postern is doubly guarded, holy father," replied Gryme with a mournful shake of the head; " and the portcullis has been lowered an hour agone. Spies are also without, their faces buried in the hoods of their cloaks; some are lingering among the cloisters, others stationed under the gateway. There is no way to escape, but in some mean disguise, and by scaling the walls, which may be done from the back windows of this building."

" And is it come to this !" said the Archbishop, with a sigh : " I, who have been attended
by hundreds of knights, gonfanons fluttering,
and trumpets sounding ; who but to-day rode
in the face of the sun, must now seek shelter
under the clouds of night, and such a night ! —
but no matter."

" It must be done," said Gryme ; " I saw the
countenances of Tracy and Fitzurse without,
and they forebode thee no good, nor would re-
sistance become thee as the head of the church,
and ruler of that kingdom which is to bring
peace, and good-will to all men ;—although there
are thousands ready to strike in thy defence."

" Thou speakest truly, good Gryme," replied
the prelate ; " but assuredly thou wouldst not
have me escape in a disguise that becometh not
my dignity, thou wouldst not have the Primate
of England wear the garb of a serf, and slink
away like a very felon.   Beside, in such a night

as this, we must be provided with steeds and attendants in case of danger."

"Not so, holy father," replied the monk, "we must depart alone, and at present on foot, and that speedily, for there is danger at hand. Our disguise must be complete, and the Primate of England wear the gaberdine of a beggar, if such will ensure his safety. And to attempt to escape in aught but the disguise of the meanest monk will, I wot well, be of none avail. I need not tell thee, holy father, that those who are now Saints in heaven, have while here below been driven into the wilderness, clothed in sackcloth, with only tears to slake their thirst, and herbs to quell their hunger. A cord and cowl must thou put on this night, if we are to escape; for on the morrow thou art doomed to fetters and the dungeon, for there are those who have for-sworn their allegiance to thee as Archbishop of

Canterbury, and are ready to treat thee as Thomas à Becket the Saxon."

"Thou speakest soothly," replied the Prelate after a long pause, and glancing at his rich dalmatica as he spoke. "The hand of Heaven moveth in these matters : even the tunic on which I trampled this morning, as being un-meet for my wearing, is now a garment too costly for the persecuted servant of Christ to put on. *Non sum qualis eram ;* bring forth the robes," said he, arising :—and rending the rich dress from his shoulders, he cast it on the floor. A faint sigh escaped his lips, as he again fell back in his seat, and as he planted his elbow on the massy arm of the chair, he rested his clouded brow on the palm of his hand; and with closed eyes and compressed lips, sat silent and motionless for several moments, and as the uncertain flames blazed, or were extinguished,

he traced in their flickering light a resemblance
to earthly honour.

For the first time he seemed to become
conscious how much he had lost by this struggle,
and how great a sacrifice he had made between
pride and conscience; but still his great soul
sunk not; and he began to contemplate the
dangers and privations which he must now
prepare himself to undergo. How much his
feeling preponderated in the balance in behalf
of the victory he had won for the church, in
whose service he had so deeply suffered, we
will not venture to scrutinize too closely. As
its head, he had waged war nobly against all
innovations; but conscience is a skittish jade;—
approach her too closely, and she will bound
aside;—hit her too hard, and she will throw you
in the mire, and prostrate you lower than you
ever were before. The Archbishop shrunk
from questioning himself too closely on these

matters. He felt like a man who has thrown a beggar a penny, when the eyes of a group of passengers were upon him, almost at a loss to know whether he had done it to be thought generous, or out of a feeling of charity. "Had he fought the battles of the church as a servant of Christ, free from every selfish feeling?—indulging no private pique,—gratifying no pride, but giving all the glory to Heaven?" The question arose in his own mind almost unawares, and he felt that he was not yet purified from all pride and selfish gratification; and there was mingled with his thoughts the remembrance that he had withstood the power of the King too much in the proud spirit of opposition.

We will not, however, entirely take away the veil, and bare every motive by which he was actuated; few hearts will stand this trial. There is more of vanity in all our natures than we wish to reveal; many motives of which we

are ourselves ignorant, and which we can only
come at by digging into the heart, and satisfying
our curiosity at the expense of great pain.
But let us do justice to the memory of the
dead. If he was weak,—he prayed to Heaven
to render him strong; and where he had erred,
resolved in future, by the help of God, to err
so no more. And few, we are bound to confess,
went under so many privations for the good of
the church as Thomas à Becket.

Look at the springs of all human actions,—
the inner wheels and hidden movements of all
we do. The eye of the patriot brightens at the
applause of his hearers; and he forgets the
miseries of his country while listening to the
shouts of the crowd. The truths of the gospel
are expounded in flowery terms, and the minister
looks around in triumph upon his smiling con-
gregation, when he has given utterance to some
new idea which he has long laboured to master.

Discretion, judgment, and caution, are but gentle terms for deceit;—candour ought ever to be armed in mail; for there are weaknesses in all our natures ready to tilt at the truth. We censure a man for his follies; when, if we examined ourselves closely, we should find that we were guilty of others equally great. But what need would there be of another and a better state of life, if we were perfect in this? or why should we not rather seek to amend, than quarrel with each other's faults? The wisest of men have dealt kindly with the frailties of our nature: it requires but little power to expose them; but to lay down plans, for their amendment, without giving pain, must be the work of a wise and kind-hearted teacher. That man who undergoes years of suffering and privation for conscience sake, deserves credit for sincerity; but he who assumes a sudden sympathy for the moment, may be doubted;—nay, even earnest passion is not always sincere; for calm and after-investigation often shows that we acted from a wrong impulse. But we cannot say so of Thomas à Becket; for he died in maintaining his opinions: and if he never was firm to his purpose in his life before, he was at the dreadful hour of death. But we are stepping beyond our story.

Gryme robed the Archbishop in the simple dress then worn by the monks of that period, which consisted of a long frock or mantle, girded at the waist by a cord, and having at the neck a hood which formed a covering for the head, and being of a piece with the garment, it could be drawn up, or thrown back in a moment, at the wearer's pleasure. The monk was also arrayed in the same costume, and, saving the difference of figure (for even in that disguise, the tall and erect form of the Arch-bishop showed to advantage) there was no

mark by which to distinguish the Primate from
his attendant. Gryme had, however, concealed
the pallium under his inner garments, for it
was not of much bulk : this Becket had received
from the Pope, on his nomination to the see
of Canterbury ; all other outward marks of his
high dignity were left behind : for the mitre, the
cross, and the rich dalmatica remained on the
floor in the same confused state as we before
described them. Becket cast his eye upon
them as he passed, and if a sigh escaped him,
it was but for a moment as he left the apartment. At a remote corner of the mansion,
stood a room which abutted from the building,
the upper window of which was on a level with
one of the walls, and not more than six feet
asunder; from this Gryme had thrust an oaken
plank, and venturing out first, he was followed
by the Archbishop, and they dropped from the
high wall in safety, for the rattling of the rain

and the roaring of the wind prevented the
sound of their footsteps from being heard by
the sentry, whose post was at some distance.
In spite of the darkness of the night (for the
moon was overcast with dark clouds), the loud
clattering of the rain, which came down in torrents, and was blown full in the face of our
travellers, Becket drew the hood closely round
his head, and they pursued their journey without a murmur, in the direction of Leicester.
If the heart of the Primate was pained at the
outset of the enterprise, and his step faltered a
moment ere he commenced his journey, both
were now firm to their purpose, for he had re-
gained all his former courage ; and as he
wrenched a huge stake from a neighbouring
hedge, and brandished it a moment in the air,
a spark of his former military spirit was kindled, and he rose with the danger, as his manly
stride increased ; and the free motion of his arm

told that long abstinence had not altogether
deprived that muscular form of its strength.
Gryme had much ado to keep pace with his
master, and was compelled every now and then
to fetch up his lost ground, by a quick trot,
like a boy who is ambitious of keeping up with
a good walker. Sometimes, however, the Primate drew in his long and rapid stride, to suit
the pace of his companion, and the latter,
already tired of the silence, thus spoke, —

" I fear me, holy father"—

" Better call me brother Dearman," said
Becket, " when you have need to use my
name ; and, on common occasions, brother
John, it will be well to sink all honours and
titles ; for the present, we must school ourselves in humility, and I am bent upon setting
thee a good example ; wherever we shelter, let
there be no distinction between us. I am
aware how thou hast, and wouldst still, serve

me, but thou must leave off thy old habits for awhile. So, brother Ambrose, come on at the bidding of brother John, both poor monks of the monastery of St. Mary's—there has been a good number of that name."

" I will endeavour to obey thee, holy father," replied Gryme, " but I fear me this journey will weary thee. But if thou canst hold out until we reach the cross at Lamport, which from North-ampton is about eight miles distant, we shall find Oswald the groom, with horses ready sad-dled for our journey; and if we halt a few mo-ments at the Scotale, at Harborough, and from thence push on at good speed, we may hope to reach Leicester by daybreak."

" Nay, fear not for me," answered the Arch-bishop, " thou shalt find brother John as good at a journey as brother Ambrose; and when once we set foot in stirrup, we will ride with the fleetest that ever run down a fallow-deer.

For thou must not forget," added he, his spirits becoming more buoyant through exercise, "that I was a soldier, and wielded the sword before I grasped the pastoral crook : and sheltered in the camp long before I had the church for a covering. But those days are gone," added he, with a sigh.

In the course of two hours' brisk walking, they reached the hamlet of Lamport ; they found Oswald in waiting beside the rude stone cross ; and after the faithful groom had knelt down with tears in his eyes, and received the Primate's blessing, they set off at a good round gallop, and having halted at the rude Scotale, or hostel, at Market Harborough, again pursued their journey. `

Towards morning, the sky became clear, and the moon looked down from her starry throne in full brilliancy, as if she only shed her silver light upon a land of peace. But the eye of

Becket caught glimpses of castles which the
fire had consumed, and of convents which the
hands of the Norman invaders had despoiled ;
for England still bore marks of the ravages
committed by William the Conqueror, and
where the village of Great Glen now stands,
the moonlight then streamed down upon a mass
of blackened ruins, for here the Saxons had
made one of their boldest stands. Sometimes
the horned owl hooted from the mouldering
turrets of a castle, which the ivy was then fast
covering, or the barking of the fox came with a
strange hollow sound from amid ruins. Here
and there, long lines of gloomy forests stretched
on either hand, and seemed to slumber after
the storm, for scarcely a sound broke the pro-
found silence, saving when some herd of dap-
pled deer brushed across the path, and for
a moment made a rustling amid the underwood; then again all was still, for only the

tramping of their steeds rang over the vast
solitude.

They journeyed along in silence, and sometimes the mind of Becket reverted to past
scenes,—to the happy days of his boyhood,—to
the deeds he had achieved when he rode armed
in mail; to the remembrance of his friendship
with Henry, his splendid embassies, his trial in
the hall but a few hours before; the looks of the
king that day, and the same look in former
times when he welcomed him to Woodstock.
Then he thought of Rosamond, and his heart
sank within him, for he well knew that during
Henry's absence, the Queen would seek by
every means to gratify her vengeance, and he
sighed deeply when he remembered that he
himself could no longer assist her, and half-
wished that he had yielded to the King for
her sake, for the Primate loved her with a
fatherly affection.

K 5

"I will yet see her," muttered he to himself, "ere I leave England; she shall not be left to perish by the machinations of that dark-minded woman, and the villain Ugglethred." And he reached Leicester in the cold grey light of an autumnal morning, revolving in his mind the best plans for obtaining an interview with Rosamond at Woodstock.

They abode all that day with a pious monk at Leicester, who had been a friend of Gryme's in former years, and towards twilight, again resumed their journey in the direction to Nottingham. They were, however, compelled to travel in bye-ways, and through roads unknown; for they heard tidings of four knights in armour, who had but a few hours before journeyed on the same road. They made a circuit along the borders of the wide forest of Charnwood,—which then extended to the very ridge of the hills, under which Mount-Sorrel

is now sheltered,—and long before daylight
they found themselves under the brow of Clifton,
the grove of which has long been celebrated in
ballad poetry. Here they halted; for the
broad river Trent was now before them, and in
consequence of the late rains, was impassable.
As no sign of either shelter or human habitation
here presented itself, they rode along by the
banks of the river for upwards of a mile, until
they came to where the village of Wilford now
stands, and which even at that early period was
known as a ferry. They reined in their steeds
beside the bank; near to which, a huge flat-
bottomed boat was moored, and was the only
communication between the opposite shores.
Beyond the river, and the broad meadows, rose
the turrets of Nottingham castle,—the huge
rock resting in half-shadow, and the straggling
town stretching along the gentle acclivity,—
here and there concealed by masses of trees,

as if it had sprung up in the midst of a forest. Looking behind them they discovered a rude shed, which was overhung by two immense oaks, and not doubting but that this was the abode of the ferryman, Becket alighted and began to knock at the door.

The deep baying of a mastiff, and the sound of a voice almost as surly, demanding the business of the intruders, were the ready answers to the Primate's summons.

" We would have thee unmoor thy boat, honest ferryman," said the Archbishop, " and give us a safe conveyance to the opposite shore."

" A safe conveyance to the devil," muttered the surly Charon; " how think you I could get across without floating down a mile or two while the stream is running at this furious rate? Go from whence you came, and disturb me not ; for I have already wafted three cursed Normans

over this very night; and the fourth, I trow, is
by this time in the safe keeping of Sathanas;
for both horse and rider went head-foremost into
the stream."

"We are no Normans, friend," replied
Gryme, "but two poor Saxon monks flying
from danger, and have need of assistance."

"The less need have ye to cross the river,"
answered the ferryman, fumbling at the wooden
bar which secured the door, and which he
opened as the broad morning broke. "Horses,
too!" added he, eyeing them narrowly; "the
one tall, and the other of middling stature;—the
very men these Norman cut-throats were en-
quiring after. Hark you, friends!" added he in
a louder tone, "I, and my fathers before me,
have kept this ferry for more than a hundred
years, and never yet defiled our hands with the
gold of the Norman. I need but to bear you
across to place you within the power of those

who are in quest of you. But if ye be Saxons, take my counsel and journey further on, for here you are halting too near the hold of the enemy; and from yonder castle all can be seen that passeth here; for the warden has the eye of an hawk."

" We thank thee for thy advice," said the Archbishop; " but having been in the saddle all night, we are but ill fitted to pursue our journey without rest and refreshment; and if it is not in thy power to grant us either, thou wilt, we trust, point out some place where we may obtain a mouthful of food, and a few hours' repose."

" Nay, an' it be thus," said the rough ferry-man, " ye shall be welcome to the best my shed affords; for it shall never be said that the son of Balder was a churl, when those of his oppressed race needed a shelter :" saying which, he led the way into his hut, having placed their horses in a rude out-house, where the steeds of his passengers were generally stabled.

"I have not been so well provisioned during the late rains," said the ferryman, producing a wooden trencher which contained a huge lump of cold fat pork, and a cake of coarse barley bread; "for but few of the good-wives venture across the river at this time of the year; but here is a stoup of Burton ale,—better never washed the lip of a saint,—and if a Saxon welcome will give this homely fare a better relish, why, in the name of St. Dunstan, fall to."

Both the guests assured their host that they needed no better fare, and Becket partook of it with a keener relish than he had before done when sharing daintier viands; for his severe abstinence had taught him to conquer trifles. Nor did the ferryman himself, when pressed to share their repast, show any reluctance; but ate with the appetite of a true Saxon, and washed it down with a cup of good ale, which the sharp smacking of his lips pronounced excellent.

Scarcely was their meal finished before they were startled by the sound of voices which came from the opposite bank of the river. " Yonder are the Norman thieves whom I ferried across ycster-even," said the ferryman, reconnoitering from a loop-hole in his shed; " I know them by their armour. The devil looketh after his own, or they would have shared the fate of their companion. It is as I feared,—the cursed warden has had a glimpse of you from the watch-tower of the castle; but fear not, the broad river will keep the blood-thirsty thieves at bay, while I plan your escape; —devil of aught shall they find but your horses."

The Primate looked through the narrow

loop-hole, and saw three men armed, and in their saddles on the opposite bank, who were riding to and fro, and hallooing at the highest pitch of their voices. The loud dashing of the river, and the sound of the wind among the trees prevented their words from being heard.

"This way," said the ferryman, hastily setting aside the remains of the meal, and opening a door at the back of his hut. He then led them round by a circuitous path, until he brought them on a line behind the banks of the river; and bidding them stoop that their heads might not be seen above the bank, led them to a considerable distance before he bade them halt.

"You are safe now," said he, pausing before a little island covered with tall osiers, which shut out all view of the opposite shore. "Steady and fear nothing, but grasp that pole firmly, and you will pass the narrow channel. Devil a bit can either man or horse reach you there, when I have unmoored the old tree, and sent it sailing down the stream." Along the hedge of the bank, and even down to the margin of the river, grew several enormous elms, some of their roots were bared by the dashing of the waters, which had from time to time carried away portions of the earth; a few were also scattered on the farthest edge of the island, and as the osiers, though leafless, were planted close together, they formed an impenetrable barrier to the eye, on the opposite shore.

Tall sedge also grew along the margin; reeds and rushes, which were white and withered, afforded safe shelter to the wild-fowl, several of which were startled from their haunts by the presence of our adventurers. The river rolled along darkly and deeply in this confined channel, and much swifter than in the broader bed of the river, and many a boiling eddy told its

strength in this narrow course ; nor did the
trunk of the extensive tree with its round side
and rough bark, that stretched across to the
island, promise too secure a footing, for in more
than one place the waves washed over it. There
was, however, no time for hesitation, for between
every pause of the wind, the voices of the
knights were heard on the opposite shore grow-
ing more angry at the delay, and roaring like
lions eager to seize their prey.

With eye firmly fixed on the end of the tree,
and the pole grasped securely in his hand,
which it required nerves of iron to hold steady
amid the furious current, the Archbishop
stepped boldly and fearlessly across in safety,
and then threw back the pole for Gryme. The
monk hesitated, and for a moment the dashing
of the stream rendered his eye unsteady, but a
word of caution from Becket made him more
calm, and although he fell all his length

amongst the tall sedge, he speedily recovered his footing, and both made their way into the very centre of the ozier-holt.

The ferryman took up the pole, and getting a purchase with it like a lever, shifted the end of the tree into the stream : it swung slowly round, until it caught the full current, and was then borne furiously down the river, and the son of Balder returned with all former caution to his hut.

CHAPTER XI.

Across the water angry voices came,
And cursed the lagging of the lazy boat;
Till dip by dip, it slow and nearer drew,
Rustled its prow along the reedy shore,
And when its keel ground on the pebbly land,
The angry Charon growled, " What want you here ?"
The Dark River.

THE sturdy ferryman was too well used to the
threats and anger of his passengers to take
much heed of them ; and when he came forth
again from the front of his hut, as if he had
but just arisen, he only replied to the impatient
shouts of the knights by a wave of his hand,
and proceeded to haul up the heavy boat against
the stream ; " and yet," muttered he to himself,
" I may as well let her drift half a mile below
the ferry, it will but be warming the blood of

yonder Norman cut-throats to haul her up again." So saying, he pushed her from the shore,—leaped in, and went drifting at a swift pace down the rapid river, without caring much to keep her head against the stream.

"The curse of every saint alight upon thee for a lazy knave!" said a knight, whose name was Reginald Fitzurse, as the ferryman drew nearer the shore; a considerable space of which they were compelled to traverse: "but I will break every bone in thy carcase the instant thou art landed."

"An' I thought thou wouldst keep thy word proud Norman, or cared the worth of a dead leaf for thy threats," replied the broad-shouldered ferryman, "thou shouldst hear the curfew toll before my keel grated on a pebble of that shore."

"Speak him fair," said another; "thou mightest have seen enough of the fellow yesternight to convince thee that he is one of those dogged Saxons who would scarce care a straw to swamp his boat, and even drown himself, so that he might rid the world of three Normans a few years before their time. Didst thou not see how the knave grinned when poor Berwin went head-foremost to the devil; cooling himself beforehand, that he might the better stand the penal flame? Speak the knave fair, or we shall have our journey for nothing."

" Gramercy for thy advice, Tracy," replied Fitzurse; " I have ever found such knaves more easily cudgelled than cajoled into sub-mission; but here he comes.—Art thou not afraid to venture within reach of us?" continued Fitzurse, making a circle with his huge cross-handled sword as he spoke, " after having kept us here bawling ourselves hoarse, and making noise enough to awaken the dead?"

" Devil a man hath set foot in my boat that

1 yet feared," replied the undaunted ferryman; " and I have given some scores a ducking in my day, who have not kept a civil tongue in their heads. As to hearing you, I make it a rule to hear no one when I am asleep; and I have already been once aroused this morning, ere I was half awake."

" Hast thou left the two monks who awoke thee safe housed ?" said Tracy.

" Monks, were they?" said the ferryman, half parrying the question ; " in truth my eyes were scarcely unclosed ; they but en- quired the way to Burton — a curse on them for wakening me — and I went to sleep again."

" Out upon thee, for a liar !" said the fiery Fitzurse ; "the warder saw them from the eastern keep enter thy shed."

" The warder drank a cup too deep," replied the ferryman, " and hath seen double this morning; and thou art a cup too low, which makes thee speak so uncivilly."

" Darest thou bandy words with me, slave?" exclaimed Fitzurse, uplifting his sword, as he was about to leap into the boat. " By the thunder of Heaven! I will cleave thee to the teeth, an' thou puttest not a bridle on thy tongue."

" An' thou pointest thy sword at me again," said the ferryman, stepping back on the shore, and uplifting the huge oar with both hands, " I will smite thee to the earth. I am no more a slave than thyself; but hold my ferry by a true grant."

" Art thou mad, Fitzurse?" said Ranulph de Broc, stepping in between them, " to stand parleying here, while our prey is already two good leagues in advance? let us overtake them; then quarrel with this fellow an' thou wilt.

Give me hold of the chain, and let us draw up
the boat against this strong current, that we
may land where there is a sure footing for our
horses." Tracy assisted him; but both being
heavily armed, they sunk up to the greaves at
every step; while Fitzurse walked along moodily
on the high embankment. Having arrived to a
sufficient height to allow for the force of the
stream in crossing, the knights seated themselves in the stern of the boat, each retaining
the reins of his steed to swim them across
the river.

The sun had by this time broke forth, and
cast his beams over the sparkling waves; while
the high rock on which the distant castle stood,
seemed bathed in a flood of light. The bright
waters went dashing around the osiered isle,
and the heart of the Primate beat quicker as
he heard the voices of his enemies nearing the
adjacent shore. The wind stole with gentle

sighs through the tall trees; then swept along the silver ripples, which chased each other in the sunshine, like children at play. The dark grove of Clifton rose high in the distance; and at the feet of its overhanging trees might be seen some solitary stag stooping to drink: it was altogether a lovely scene. The prow of the boat cut its way through the dashing waters, as the armour of the knights flashed back the rays of the sun, and the horses snorted as they breasted the waves; while the rude hut of the ferryman, with its thatched roof, green with moss, or grey with lichen,— all combined to form such a picture as a Calcott could have transferred to canvass, and rivetted down the eye of the beholder for hours.

At length the boat drew up to where the long grass swayed idly to and fro along the shore, and the men-at-arms alighted. " I will not take this knave's word," said Fitzurse, looking

into the ferryman's hut to satisfy himself that
there was no one there, and adding, " methinks
it would not be amiss to scour yonder thicket
on the eminence."

" Hast thou spoken truly on this matter?" said
Ranulph de Broc, presenting the boatman with
a gold piece. " If thou knowest aught of the
place of concealment of these monks," added
he, looking narrowly into the broad hard face
of the ferryman, " and wilt guide us to it, ten
of these gold pieces shall be thine?   Hark thee,
friend! under one of these monkish guises is
hidden the Archbishop of Canterbury,—the
traitor Thomas à Becket."

" Had you told me this yesternight," answered the ferryman, his countenance undergoing no alteration, " I might have landed
them in the opposite meadows; then you need
only to have made a sally from the lower
postern, and captured them at leisure."

" 'Twere well an' I had made thee master of
this secret," said De Broc ; " but we dreamed
not of their following so near in our steps.
They kept not the course below the wood ?"
enquired he.

" The path beyond the grove is the only safe
bridle-way," replied the son of Balder. " When
ye have ridden beyond Barton, you will reach
another ferry, and find the opposite banks the
better pathway."

" To horse !" exclaimed Ranulph de Broc ;
and the knights leaped nimbly into their saddles,
in spite of their cumbrous armour; and the
clattering of their chargers' hoofs soon sounded
in the distance.

" Spur on, ye bloody-minded villains," said the
ferryman, jerking the gold piece into the river,
which leaped from ripple to ripple, as if loth to
sink. " I will not defile my pouch with your
cursed coin.   And yet," added he, his eye fixed

upon the spot where it sank, " it is folly to fling away one's hire, when it might have made light the heart of some poor serf. Alice of the Grove could have purchased new gaberdines for her four naked urchins, and found them food for three moons besides. But, no matter, it is gone ; and I vow to her as good a piece in its stead.—Archbishop of Canterbury ! well, he is a Saxon, and has spoken truth, and may remember me in his prayers for this deed, and, mayhap, offer up a mass or two for the soul of my father. But, what doeth he in this guise ?" continued he, as he again secured his boat to the post, and so conjecturing a thousand things, he again entered his hut.

Meantime, the persecuted Primate and his faithful attendant were safely sheltered in the cold osier bed, which, but a few days before, was under water, and was now ancle-deep in wet weeds, or spongy and sinking soil. Becket had seated himself on a large dead root, which had been thrown aside to burn, and Gryme rested upon a pile of withered peelings, which smoked in the morning sunshine.

"These are trials that we must learn to endure," said the Primate, as he watched the monk securing the strings of his shoes, from which he had been emptying the water: "it is useless to sit with folded arms and head bent, sighing over our sorrows ; we must learn to bear troubles without murmuring, and to travail on under the burthen of our griefs patiently."

"Thou shalt not find me the first to complain," said Gryme, coughing, as if he had already caught a severe cold: "I would fain wear out this old body of mine in thy service, for it can never undergo a worthier trial."

"Fortune plays strange freaks with us," continued the Archbishop, following the tenor of his thoughts, without hearing the monk's reply, " I but little deemed, when my ears were stunned with the shouts of the assembled populace in the streets of Northampton, that I should so soon have to seek shelter in solitudes like these—have to sit and listen to the whispering of the wind, and the plashing of the river, and wander like an outcast upon the face of the earth." He rested his brow in the palm of his hand as he spoke, and remained several moments in silence. " But it hath ever been so," continued he ; " the brave Vortigern was a king one day, and the next a slave in chains ; even the high-minded Alfred had to seek shelter in the hut of a neat-herd, and superintend the baking of bread. A few years since and England flourished beneath the sway of the Saxons ; then came the Danes, and wrenched it from their grasp ; then the Norman Conqueror swept like a fierce hurricane through the land, leaving traces of his desolating march in every town and hamlet; and no one but Death was mighty enough to wrench the sceptre from his grasp. One stroke of fate makes the monarch a menial; the bishop a beggar. A few blows of the sword, and the Saxon lords became serfs, and the meanest Norman who ever held the stirrup of the squire, in one day became a baron."

" It is too true," replied Gryme, " but, hark! I heard some one call." It was the voice of the ferryman.

" How now?" said Becket, " we heard the tramping of their steeds; may we resume our journey without danger ?"

" There is no fear for the present, holy father," said the boatman, speaking in a more deferential tone than he had before assumed, " an' ye can but catch this rope, and draw this huge plank across, which I have long had con-

L 5

cealed under the bank in case of danger, you may again resume your journey, for I have sent the hounds in a wrong slot."

This was speedily done, and offered a safer footing than the slippery tree; and as the water was now much smoother, they passed over without difficulty.

"I have sent a boy with your horses, by a secret path to Shelford," continued the ferry-man; "and by taking the course up yonder lane for a mile or two, you will then find an open pathway, which will lead you to the hamlet where your steeds are in waiting; and from thence by winding ways, sometimes by the river, and along the brow of the hills you will reach Newark, to which place, if I understand aright, your journey bends."

Becket tendered his thanks for the good services which he had received, and offered the honest ferryman two gold pieces, which the

latter refused, saying, " No, holy father, I have
to crave pardon for the rude reception you met
with at my hands this morning, and if I am
not unworthy, would fain share your blessing
ere you depart; and if, when you again are engaged in your holy calling, (which may the
Holy Virgin speedily bring about!) I would beg
that your reverence remember the soul of Balder
the boatman of the Trent, and let these few
gold pieces be expended in masses at the high
altar of Canterbury."

"Thy wishes shall be obeyed, my son," replied the prelate, "for the services thou hast
this day done me. But put up thy gold; it
shall not be needed."

The ferryman knelt down, and received the
Primate's blessing, then departed with a lighter
heart than he had felt for many a day.

They reached Shelford, and found their horses
in readiness, and again resumed their journey

along the beautiful borders of the Trent. Where
now many a village slopes down to the sweet
water-edge, then only grew wild masses of
underwood, — and stretched immense tracts of
forest-land, which plough had never disturbed,
nor had their echoes been broken by the sound
of the woodman's axe. Glen and glade slumbered in the same wild grandeur as when the
wolf made its lair there, and the wild boar
ground its tusks upon the bolls of the knotted
oaks. Along the opposite shore stretched
the gloomy forest of Sherwood, which in
those days extended to the very verge of the
river; herds of deer were standing under the
giant oaks, and the otter darted to and fro in
quest of its finny prey; while at some arm of
the river might be seen the shallop of a fisher-
man gliding along in the sunshine, for it was
one of those days that brings back summer into

the lap of autumn. They halted at a scot-ale in Stoke, then an extensive village, and reached the old town of Newark before night-fall; where they rested at the monastery of St. Winifred, the Abbot of which was friendly to the cause of Becket. Next day they pursued their course over the sandy and marshy plains of Lincoln-shire, for where Long Collingham, and all those lengthy villages now stretch, not a hamlet was seen until they came to Torksey, the mouth of the old Roman Fossdyke; nor any human habitation saving the lonely hut of some war-rener. At Torksey they left their horses, and pursued their way on foot by the ancient water-course, to the already far-famed city of Lincoln, along a path which the foot-beaten traveller contemplates with horror in the present day; for even now it is only one weary waste of heavy sand-banks, overgrown with stunted brambles

and armies of thistles, varied by low planta-
tions of dwarf firs, and the gibbet post of a
murderer, whose bones have long since moul-
dered away.

CHAPTER XII.

The swarthy Smith spits in his buck-horn fist,
And bids the man bring out the five-fold twist,
His shackles, shacklocks, hampers, gyves, and chains;
And if a carrier's jade be brought unto him,
His man can hold his foot whilst he can shoe him.
BROWNE's *Pastorals.*

THE brief Autumn day was fast drawing to a close, when our travellers came in sight of the ancient city of Lincoln; and long and dreary seemed the distance, when after journeying a mile or two on the loose sands that banked in the Roman Fossdyke, they seemed to be no nearer to the huge cathedral, which had so long been visible from its proud eminence. Becket paused a moment to gaze upon the mighty building, which like a huge Titan seemed to bestride the hill, and overlook the old city which sloped away from its feet: its huge towers and rich windows were bathed in the deep crimson of sunset, which also shed a dusky and ominous lustre over the lower streets of the city. Ever and anon the deep-toned bell of the cathedral sent forth its slow and measured knell over the wide waste of marshes, and was answered by the booming of some solitary bittern from the sedge, or the shrill shrieking of the curlew. The Primate sat down upon the bank of the Fossdyke, while Gryme unloosed the thongs which secured his shoes, for they had become painful through the quantity of loose sand which they now contained; and as his eye fell upon the calm surface of the stream, he forgot his pain for a moment, while his imagination called up the gilded galleys of the Romans, which more than a thousand years agone had ploughed up those tranquil waters.

"Here," said he, addressing Gryme in a me-

lancholy tone of voice, "still stands the work
of the conquerors of the world, the remains of
fallen power, the watery way which the Romans
made to connect the broad Trent with the waves
of the Witham, that their galleys might ride
safely from river to river. Yes, even here,"
continued he, "has the tramp of the Roman
cohorts been heard; and the proud eye of Julius
Cæsar, as he stood on the prow of his vessel,
glanced at their armed ranks, as they bore the
eagle aloft, and marched in triumph to yonder
city. Alas! Gryme," added he, his thoughts
instantly changing, "how brief a space of time
is it since I myself was heralded into those
walls, amid the sounding of trumpets, and the
loud acclaim of voices; when my long train of
followers filled the whole line of its hilly streets,
and the King of Scotland helped me to alight
from my saddle. And now I go to seek a
night's shelter, and crave a mouthful of food,

where before I ———." He buried his face in his hands, and sat several moments without speaking a word.

"Take comfort, holy father," replied the faithful monk: "God, in his own good time, will avenge thy wrongs. Remember that the blessed Saviour himself was a wanderer in the wilderness, and that many of the Saints who are now in heaven, underwent persecution: travelled bare-footed from place to place, bore cold and hunger, and cruel scourgings; and all for the Church's sake. Come, let us pursue our course; we shall find some one, who, for the love of God, will give us food and shelter;—there is yet many a kind heart beating amid the green hills and wide valleys of England."

"And Rosamond!" continued Becket, arising and continuing his course along the deep sandy path: "Thou knowest not, Gryme, how my heart yearneth towards her, and how my conscience smiteth me, when I remember that I was instrumental in bringing about her ill-fated marriage."

"Let not that grieve you, reverend father," replied the monk; "the King treateth her with kindness and great love; and sad regrets cannot alter the past, no more than human fore-sight can prevent future ills from befalling us."

"True, true," said the Primate in the same melancholy voice: "Henry loveth her, and that is some consolation; I too, have a fatherly affection for her. Yes," added he, musing, "I will still remain true to my pledge; but one word from my lips, Gryme, would make her England's Queen, and drive the dark-minded Eleanor again to her own dominions."

"But these matters could not be achieved without much bloodshed, reverend father," answered the monk; "and from your own lips I am taught to believe that the change would make the Lady Rosamond no happier."

" Thou speakest sooth," replied the Prelate ; " but I can tell thee that the revengeful queen will never rest until she hath imbued her hands in the blood of her fair rival. And it will need a vigilant watch to keep her vengeance aloof."

The shades of evening were by this time falling, for they had now reached that wide part of the Fossdyke, known in the present day by the name of Braford, which comes up to within a short distance of the principal street of the city. They halted beside the shop of a blacksmith, and Gryme entered the dusky smithy to enquire the nearest way to the convent of St. Mary.

The smith himself, a fine muscular fellow, with his huge brawny arms bared to the shoulders ; and his soiled leather doublet and apron of the same material, bearing the marks of much toil and long service,—was busied in beating out a horse-shoe when the monk entered, and drawing his bulky body erect, and wiping the perspiration from his brow on his sinewy arm, he gazed on the countenance of Gryme without replying, while the Cyclop who aided this ancient Vulcan, took the advantage of the pause, and leant upon the huge hammer which he had been wielding, to rest himself. Becket stood without, and as the twilight was now fast approaching, the deep ruddy glare from the forge streamed full upon his fine but melancholy countenance, making such a picture as the eye of an artist loves to dwell upon.

"St. Mary's, St. Mary's," said the smith; "the city gates will be closed ere this, and" turning to his Cyclop, he added, "Swaine, give the Abbot's horse a little hay, and shake up its bed for the night; and remember that the charge of his provender is added to the shoeing when he is fetched on the morrow." The attendant retired to obey his master's commands. He then continued : " the drawbridge is never lowered after sunset, and all the sallyports in the Roman wall are closed at the ringing of curfew, and"—he had hitherto kept his eye stedfastly upon Gryme, and having observed that Swaine was now out of sight, he threw his hammer upon the floor, and seizing the hands of the monk between his own " buckhorn fists," exclaimed, " Have you forgotten Turstin, the son of Stur, who threw aside his breviary to take up the hammer and tong, like St. Dunstan ?"

" Mine old acquaintance," echoed the monk, kissing the grimy cheek of the smith, the ancient mode of English salutation ; " and how fares it with thee, since thou hast shown the convent a clean pair of heels ?"

" I can scarcely tell thee," replied the smith,
overjoyed at thus meeting with an old acquaintance ; " but thou rememberest when I
broke my vow and my head at the same time.
I then betook me to this honest trade (not
but that a priest's is a worthy profession), but
I ever, as thou knowest, loved the ale-cup
better than the chalice, and a bear-baiting
beyond my books ; so I took to myself a
wife, having confessed her beforehand, got a
quittance from the worthy Prior ; and here I
am as thou now seest me."

Gryme cast his eye upon Becket, who had
by this time entered the shed, and the monk
would rather that Turstin had confined his
narrative to his own ears ; but the mischief
was done ; so, without further preface, he began
to inquire where they might find a lodging for
the night ?

" And where should it be ?" replied the smith,

who had so candidly avowed his backsliding from the Church, "but under the roof of an honest Saxon like yourself, who will endeavour to make up his lack of piety by his best fare, and think himself well rewarded if you mention his name in your prayers, for you was always what you seem," added the smith, with a sigh, "and it was in vain my trying to become what I was not born to. I learnt to deal heavy blows at a morrice, or a May-day meeting, before I dealt them upon hot iron."

" And my companion," continued Gryme, " he also hath need of shelter and privacy for a short time; for, to deal plainly with thee, we are flying from danger, and know not how soon it may overtake us."

" Shelter and food he shall gladly have with me for thy sake," answered the man of iron, subduing his free tone of conversation; for he was now struck for the first time by the noble appearance of the Primate, who had not lost a jot of that innate dignity which was so habitual to his character, " shelter and food, and such safety as the humble roof and strong arm of a poor Saxon can afford him."

" I thank thee, friend," replied the Archbishop, " I am also a Saxon, and will do as much for thee and thine, shouldst thou ever have the ill fortune to be as hard-bested as myself, which may Heaven forbid."

The honest blacksmith made a low genuflection, muttered his answer in tones which were inaudible; and, entering a low doorway which communicated with his shop and dwelling-house, departed to make arrangements for his guests. The Primate of England folded his arms, and seated himself on the iron anvil, while the monk stood warming his benumbed hands over the fire; and here we must leave them to their conversation, while we take a

survey of the household of Turstin, the son of
Stur, the trusty blacksmith of Lincoln.

The door by which the smith entered, opened
into a long low apartment, the roof of which
was blackened with smoke ; at one corner
blazed a huge fire of wood ; and as the room
contained no chimney, and the wind blew in
at a kind of loop-hole or window, which opened
above the flames, the smoke rolled back in deep
drifts, and filled the apartment. Around the
walls, which were chiefly formed of wood, hung
numerous horse-shoes of almost all sizes, and
various pieces of timber, which seemed placed
there to season, and be in readiness for future
hammer-shafts and other tools ; but an expe-
rienced eye might detect the rude outlines of
future cross-bows and straight shafts, for the
smith was not a man to tie himself to any
particular craft. Two or three huge logs of
wood stood ready for seats, and two stools, the

tops of which were just as rough as when sawn
from the cross-grain of the tree ; each, however,
stood upon three rough ash-pole legs, on
which the bark remained ; the top was bound
round with hoops of iron to keep them from
splitting ; but it behoved any one, before
sitting upon them, to see that each leg was in
its proper place. A table, which had once been
a door, and was now elevated after the manner
of the stools, stood in the centre of the room ;
over this was suspended an iron lamp, of the
smith's own making, the blaze of which was
nearly obscured by the smoke.

Before the fire sat the mistress of this murky
mansion, watching the progress of the evening meal, which, suspended by a chain,
was simmering in an iron pot ;—two dirty
children were quarrelling in the midst of the
floor, and one having struck the other, on the
head with an iron shoe, had just received

M 2

punishment from the hard hand of the mother, and was bawling in chorus with his brother. At the end of the room was reared a ladder which gave access to the floor above through a hole in the roof. The smoke,—the squalling of the children, — together with the dull red and flickering light of the lamp, and a kind of oily or smoky stench,—bore little promise of making the sojourn of our travellers very desirable.

" Thou needed not to have left off thy work yet," said the wife, catching a side glimpse at her husband; " the souse is not ready; and what with the bairns bawling, and the fuel being damp, and the pot having slipped aside and almost put the fire out, I'm half distracted."

" Patience, wife! patience!" said the burly smith, I trust thou wilt not be in thy tantarums to-night; for there are two guests in the smithy that we must give a meal's meat, and a night's shelter to, and—"

"Some lazy monks or other, I'll warrant," answered this rib of iron. "Marry! thou mayest work;—all these bone-idle fellows find thee out. But I should not matter it so much, an' they needed it; but when I think of their tithes, and their orchards, and their cattle, and their fish-ponds, and the money they have paid for masses, and—"

"No matter dame," said the husband, breaking in upon his wife's conversation; for as he was wont to say, when her tongue once got loose, it went like a lamb's tail. "They have spoken many a good word for us; and I never knew a kind turn lost. Beside, one of them looks like an abbot or a prior, so we know not what he may do for us; the other is an old acquaintance of mine; and beshrew me, if I would not share my last crust with him."

" A bonny place for an abbot to come to,"
answered the wife. " There is the Minster
above the hill, where the bishop eats from off
silver and gold; and we have but three wooden
platters, and four vessels of clay, which Peter
the potter ought to have been ashamed to turn
out of his hands so rough and unfinished. Well,
well! an' ye have left this great man in your
shop, and never a cask nor a log for him to sit
down upon. Begone Turstin! and send in
Swaine to aid me in looking after the souse;
and when I ding against the partition with a
shoe, ye may then bring them in."

Turstin, the son of Stur, obeyed; and again
entered the smithy, and Gryme thus resumed
the conversation which he had been carrying on
with the archbishop. " Couldst thou not favour
us with a safe shelter for a day or two?" said
Gryme; " I know thou art to be trusted; and
if thou couldst but conceal my reverend com-

panion, I could take a hand at the forge if any one chanced to call; thou mightest find something for me to hammer at; or I might keep up the blast of the furnace; we should escape suspicion here, better than if we abode at any of the monasteries."

" That hand of thine would tell tales, worthy Gryme," said the smith, bringing the fire to a blaze as he spoke, and spreading out his broad black hand; " No; we may, an' ye like, keep you both safe enough in our own loft: but were you to take up a hammer, there are so many who come in to point a nail, or borrow a rasp, that they would laugh at your smithcraft, and say that Turstin had got a help to shoe hogs in place of horses,—a smith whose blows would scarce bring down a butterfly; and we should have all the gossips of Lincoln hanging about the doorway, from Tim the lazy troubadour, to Bernard the bear-ward."

" It would need some caution to pass for one of thy craft," said the archbishop, taking hold of the buck-horn fist of the smith, and examining it as a geologist would the paw of an antediluvian lizard ; while his own long white fingers looked like a row of bright pins, laid side by side, with an equal number of rough hob-nails ; " these hands have been acquainted with something heavier than bead and book, and I doubt not but that thou art as happy," added he, heaving a sigh, " while earning thy bread by the sweat of thy brow, as if thou faredst sumptuously, and spent thy days in a palace."

" I have no cause to murmur, holy father," answered the honest smith, proud at the notice bestowed upon him by a man of Becket's appearance ; " I have got a name that is now famous through all this shire ; for I have found out a secret to temper my nails ; and Walter of Washinbro' lames ten horses to my one ;—

it is through making them soft, your reverence," added he, taking up a huge horse-nail between his finger and thumb and bending it over his nose; " this is the test of a good nail; for it will drive aside sooner than lame a steed. But I hear the summons for supper, and will now gladly make you welcome to the best my humble shed affords."

Becket smiled at the simple egotism of the blacksmith, and followed him into the inner apartment. Gryme exchanged a look with his master, when their eyes had glanced over the humble board; for Becket was placed at the end of the table or door, and took his seat upon the empty cask; the monk sat beside the smith, —Swaine, the help or journeyman, sat opposite, —the two children standing on either side of him, their heads just level with the board,— while the hostess faced the Primate. Before her stood a huge pewter vessel filled with souse,

—an old Saxon dish consisting of the offal of swine, ears and hocks, etc., with which kale was boiled, and to an hungry man, offering no bad supper; barley-cakes were placed beside the trencher of each guest;—Swaine and the smith had, however, two earthen vessels which resembled the stands of flower-pots; two rusty knives and a wooden spoon, were all that the table presented ; while the salt was placed in a hole of the board, cut, beyond doubt for the purpose. Although etiquette in those days was unknown amongst the lower classes, and such a hard word had never been heard, yet the wife of Turstin first pushed the pewter vessel up to Swaine, that he might send it towards the Primate ; but Swaine, only bent upon satisfying his own hunger — which was somewhat of the keenest, as the evening meal had been prolonged beyond the usual hour—seized a pig's ear with his hand,—took a pinch of salt between his thumb and finger, and then fishing out a large hock, with which he burnt his fingers,—he thrust the dish away with one hand, and crammed the scalded finger into his mouth. While the Archbishop was helping himself, both the children made a snatch at Swaine's plate, and one seized the ear, and the other the hock, then down they squatted upon the floor.

" Thou art served aright," said the hostess to Swaine; " and wilt have to wait for thy greediness."

" Peace, wife !" growled Vulcan, and the Cyclop muttered something to himself; but the dish had speedily traversed the table, and all was again quiet; for each ate with a relish that only true hunger knows. A horn of good ale was handed round; and although all had to drink from the same cup, it was swallowed with as much pleasure as if it had thrown its white foam around a rim of gold.

After supper the Archbishop had to listen to an account of his own embassy to Lincoln,—for the wife of Turstin had witnessed that gorgeous procession, and soon grew warm in describing it; and although her narrative might amuse our readers—for it even caused a smile to gather on the care-worn countenance of the Primate, as he listened to a description of himself,—yet we must withhold it from them; having already too long delayed the progress of our story in following the course of the archbishop. The smith resigned his own pallet to the Primate, and clean straw was scattered in a corner of the loft for Gryme; while Turstin and his family passed the night on the floor of the lower room, and Swaine took up his station in an outer shed or stable. The eyes of the prelate were soon closed in slumber; and although visions of former splendour, mingled with the ferryman's hut, and the smith's shed, and the forge seemed to stand beside the altar at Canterbury, and the voices of the priests were broken by the hammering of the anvil; yet, when he was awakened next morning by the clattering of the smith, he found himself wonderfully refreshed.

CHAPTER XIII.

And even there, his eye being big with tears,
Turning his face, he put his hand behind him,
And with affection wondrous sensible,
He wrung Bassanio's hand, and so they parted.
SHAKSPEARE.

WITHOUT dwelling longer upon the narrow escapes, adventures, and privations, of the Archbishop and his faithful attendant, we need but simply state that they quitted the honest blacksmith in safety, were afterwards compelled to shelter with a hermit, on a lonely island amid the wide waters of Lincolnshire; and, after remaining there three days, often

suffering through both cold and hunger, they
again reached the Cathedral of Canterbury.
Amid the vaults and winding passages of this
venerable pile Becket found a secure shelter;
and it is on record that he caused an aperture
to be made between his hiding-place and the
church, that he might hear mass; and although
his secret was known to most of the monks, not
one was base enough to betray him, so highly
was his character estimated amongst the brethren of his order. More than one opportunity
had offered him a clear escape from England;
but still he lingered in the hopes of obtaining an interview with Rosamond, for he was
well aware of the machinations of Eleanor;
and, as he himself had been in a great measure
the chief mover of her marriage with Henry, he
felt anxious for her safety. A chance at last
presented itself; for Henry was busied in

searching the rich manor of Berkhamstead, one of the Prelate's splendid residences—for the King had seized upon all Becket's possessions—and, while he was thus employed, the Primate reached Oxford secretly ; and, having apprised Rosamond of his near presence, he only waited the coming of night, to obtain the long-desired interview.

Night came, as the darkness of Autumn threw its shadow upon the gloomy brow of Winter, for the year was now fast waning ; and, followed by Gryme, the Prelate entered the wild chase of Woodstock. The moon had not yet arisen ; and they pursued their course along the darksome paths of the park in silence, every avenue of which was as familiar to Becket in the noon of night as in the broad blaze of day.

" Here," thought the Primate, as his steed

paced leisurely along, " I have wandered with Henry ;—at this spot we have often parted ;—I to carry his greetings to Rosamond before meeting him at the banquet.   In this very avenue did his word put me in the power of immense possessions, which he is now depriving me of.   Here we have walked alone and talked over the affairs of state,—laid down plans for the peace of England,—plotted the overthrow of some tyrannical Norman,—opened our hearts to each other as if we had been brothers.   Have these thoughts then never passed through his own mind when he has wandered by these scenes ?   But what would it avail me to know ; he refused me the kiss of peace, and we shall never be what we were to each other again."

" Our power hath greatly faded," said he; addressing the monk, " since we last journeyed through these scenes.   We dreamed not then

that, like the hart in the thicket, we should
have to hide ourselves from the hunters,—be
exposed to cold and hunger, and all those privations which we have since undergone. But
they will one day have an ending," added he,
heaving a deep sigh ; "the weary will at last find
rest, and friend and foe lie down, and take their
long sleep together. Death decides all quarrels:
—the grave is a final peacemaker ; and there all
grievances are hushed."

"All suffer not like ourselves," replied
Gryme; "remember, holy father! that it is
some consolation to think that all thou hast
undergone, and art still undergoing, is for the
glory of the church of Christ."

"Glory is but a shadow, Gryme!" answered
the Primate in a solemn voice. "Fame and
ambition are sounds that deceive us! there is
nothing great but pure piety, and real humility!

Glory is but a sound! and men deceive the world and dishonour themselves to appear great! The coward would be thought brave,—the thief would fain have the world believe him honest,—the man who accumulates riches by grinding down the poorest serfs, makes a display of generosity before his equals,—the hypocrite assumes a holiness which he possesses not,—and justice makes a display of impartiality, which is sold the next moment to the highest bidder. Gryme, we deceive ourselves; there is something selfish and dishonest in the best of us; we do not suffer and endure for the sake of righteousness alone. If we make a sacrifice for that which is good, we listen for the applause of the world, and point out the deed that we may receive the praise of men. Shall I tell thee that I have felt the glowing pride pervade me when I have thought, that future ages will look upon me as a martyr for what I have suffered."

" Thou lookest into the human heart too deeply," reverend father, replied Gryme. " If our natures were freed from all these weaknesses, what need would there be of vigils, prayer, and penance, when we should at once be fit for the assembly of the saints ?"

" But thinkest thou, that with these feelings we are fit to loose and bind ?" continued Becket, " to take upon our shoulders the sins of others, when we ourselves have enough to bow us down to the earth,—that our ears which are open to the evils of others, do not turn to our own,—and have the most need of that mercy which we hold out to those who fly to us for succour ?　Gryme, I tell thee that these thoughts have haunted me much of late.　We who stand between the mercy of Heaven and the crimes which are opened before us, have need to be as pure in heart as the angels. We assume a sanctity which we possess not; and lay claim to a power which is in the hands of God alone. We deceive others; while we ourselves go astray with open eyes."

"These are matters which I understand not aright, holy father," answered the monk; "and which but few in the church, saving yourself, have inquired into."

"Thou sayest sooth," replied Becket; "our creed is bowed down beneath bolts and shackles, and none must unloose her; she is made a prisoner to customs and forms, and no one bringeth her to trial. The fold of Christ is guarded by sleepy shepherds; if the wolf stealeth in without making an alarm they care not, so that he disturbeth not the next on watch. The Church is filled with lazy drones who

labour not, they sleep and eat; then wake to
sleep again, as if they were but born to consume
so much food, pass so many days upon the earth,
then creep into their graves to be forgotten.
They are of no more use than the figures in an
arras, which move to and fro when the wind
bloweth, then fall again into their usual folds,
and remain still.   They amble the marked mile
to the well, and will not bestir themselves to
make a new path, when the waters of Truth
might be obtained within half the distance.
But the day will come when Truth will be
stripped of all her barbarous trappings,—when
the clear walls of her temple will be bared, and
all the beautiful tracery revealed, without the
cumbrous curtaining which is now thrown over
it.   That day we shall never live to see."

So they pursued their journey through the
gloomy avenues of the park, the soul of Becket

teeming with aspirations worthy of a more enlightened age; for his clear mind saw through
the feeble mist which surrounded the vatican,
and he revolted at the suggestions of the Pope,
who had long ago wished him to keep on fair
terms with the King at any sacrifice. At length
he reached the entrance of the labyrinth, and
leaving the faithful monk to take care of the
steeds in a neighbouring thicket, the Primate
threaded the intricate but well-known mazes
alone in the darkness.

Pierre de Vidal kept watch in a kind of
cavern at the innermost verge of the winding
passages, and as he stepped out to receive
Becket, of whose coming he was apprised by
his fair mistress, the eye of the Archbishop
caught a glance at Gamas Gobbo, who, coiled
up like a dog, lay fast asleep on a bear-skin
before the fire. Becket entered the apartment,

into which we have before conducted our readers,
and Rosamond threw herself at his feet to im-
plore his blessing.

" Arise, my daughter," said the Prelate;
" and invoke not sinful dust, that hath more need
of the aid of Heaven than thyself. I have ever
breathed forth a blessing for thee in my prayers,
which I trust the Holy Virgin hath accepted."

" I thank thee, holy father," said Rosamond,
arising and seizing the Prelate's hands, " thou
hast ever been as a father to me; and I but pray
to live to see thee once more reconciled to the
King, then I could die happy."

" Alas! there is a great gulph between us,"
replied Becket, " which neither of us can again
pass; the heart once estranged, my dearest
daughter, never returneth again with its former
freshness. It was the will of Heaven that we
should become divided."

" And Rosamond ever after remain unhappy,"
added she with a sigh, which shook her very
heart.

" I am about to leave England," continued
Becket, " perhaps for ever;—can I be of any
service to thee ere I depart? Thou art one of
the very few my heart leaves behind with
regret; and for thy sake, more than my own,
I have often wished that there was no division
between myself and his Highness."

" I shall not need earthly aid much longer,
holy father," answered Rosamond, in a low,
sweet, yet melancholy voice. " My life has
been but one continued scene of trouble, and
it will, ere long, draw to a close. Would that
my dying eyes might behold yourself and
Henry the friends that you once were, ere they
set in eternal darkness !"

"That can never be again," replied Becket

in a mournful tone. " It is useless casting our eyes upon the past, let us look forward to amend the future. Were I to throw myself at Henry's feet, he would never take me to his heart again, but would scorn me the more for my humility."

" Nay, you think too harshly of his nature, reverend father," said Rosamond; " he even now applauds your high spirit, and regrets your privations; it is those around him who feed the flames which have blazed out between you; if left alone, they would soon become extinguished."

" It is but the spark of the warrior that is kindled in my favour," answered Becket: " the bravest knight who meets his mortal foe in the lists respects his valour, while he hates him. But let him once sue like a coward for mercy, and he would tread upon him like a reptile, and crush him beneath his armed heel. No! I will not call down his scorn; he shall find in me a foe worthy of combating."

As he thus spoke, his eyes kindled with their ancient military ardour; and he looked more like a warrior about to enter the lists, than one who had spent his late days in penitence and prayer.

"Rosamond," continued he, in his most endearing tone, "let me see thee in some place of safety ere I depart; I have a strange foreboding that if I leave thee here, exposed to the machinations of the crafty Eleanor, we shall never meet again. Consider thine own safety ere it is too late."

"It must not be," replied Rosamond; "here will I abide my fate,—come when it will, it shall be welcome." A tear stole unawares down her cheek as she spoke.

"But thou art surrounded with danger," continued the Archbishop ;—"what can tempt thee to remain in a place where thy very life is menaced? How art thou now protected?"

"Thy holy office, reverend father," said Rosamond, heaving a deep sigh, "preventeth thee from feeling as a woman feels; thou hast not the weakness to love."

"It may be that I have not now," replied Becket; "but there was a time when my heart was as much a slave to this passion as thine own. But that time has gone. Thinkest thou that I, who have the hot eastern blood dashing through my veins, have never worshipped at the altar of thy sex. Ah! and shivered a lance in behalf of the beauty of her I had chosen; but I have long ago torn these feelings from my heart."

"I have heard thy mother named as a woman

possessing great charms," said Rosamond;
" a beauty that belongeth not to the cold
North. Something too have I heard of the
strange adventure of her love, but with too
great a minglement of romance in the narrative; but I have never heard the story from
thy lips."

" I will tell it thee," answered Becket,—
" briefly and truly. I have nought to boast of
in my father's birth, saving that he went out
with the crusaders and fought for the holy
sepulchre; but little dreaming that on a future
day his son would be called upon to fight the
battles of the Holy Church with spiritual
weapons. He became the captive of an Emir,
and after having languished in captivity for
above twelve moons, at length found favour in
the sight of the Infidel, and was admitted to his
table. The Emir's daughter loved my father;

nor, although a heathen, could he behold her
beauty without emotion. They conversed together, she planned his escape, and by her aid
he reached England in safety. But she loved
too well to stay long behind him ; and disguis-
ing herself, and taking with her her most costly
jewels, she set out for the sea-coast, and finding
a vessel that was about to sail for England,
she embarked. I have heard her dwell upon
the perils of her voyage; and afterwards she
learned that it was owing to the bravery of a
knight who was returning from the holy wars
that she escaped, or the crew would have mur-
dered her for her wealth. She reached England, remembering only the names of " London"
and " Gilbert," the only English words that
she could utter ; and when she arrived in London, she wandered day after day from street
to street, wringing her hands, and exclaiming,

"Gilbert, Gilbert." She at length by chance reached the street in which my father lived; who seeing a crowd assembled, ventured forth to inquire into the matter, and there he beheld the lovely heathen, seated on a stone in the street, ready to sink through very weariness. Her eyes no sooner fell upon him than she sprang into his arms, and was borne senseless into the house. She became a Christian, and my father's wife; and I, their son, sprang from a crusader and a Saracen. Thus, lady, you have the whole history in a few words."

"This was indeed love," said Rosamond, heaving a sigh; "nor have I, in giving up my fair fame for ever, made so great a sacrifice as the Saracen maiden; she gave up her home, her country, and the faith of her fathers for love. I have but given up my good name and

my heart; but," added she with a sigh, " I resigned them where I loved."

Becket gazed on her anxiously as she spoke,
and there was a tenderness in his deep-set eye,
such as seldom lingered there; and when her
eye met his, he turned suddenly away, and
paced the vaulted chamber with rapid strides.
" Rosamond," said he, at length halting before
her, and speaking under great excitement, " I
know not what hath led me to this visit. My
heart hath long yearned towards thee, even as if
thou hadst been mine own daughter. I never
look upon thee without conjuring up the image
of my mother, (may Heaven assoil her!)—like
what she was when I climbed her knee, a child.
Fairer thou art, and hast not her dark hair;
but oh! thy features are very like her own,—
and the sound of thy voice is the same as that
which soothed me when I was a child. I had

also a sister, but she died when young; thy lips and features also resemble hers. I know not why, but thou art very dear to me; thy own father could not love thee with a deeper, or purer love than that which I bear for thee." He paused a few moments, for his voice faltered through the deep emotion under which he laboured, while Rosamond passed her hands over her lovely face and wept bitterly. " I leave England," continued he, " with the dawn of day; and what grieveth me even more than my quarrel with the King, is, that I leave thee in danger. Wilt thou escape with me?—I will be to thee a father, and thou shalt be unto me as a child."

A silence still as death, and almost as awful, reigned in the chamber for several moments, broken only at intervals by the deep sobs that escaped from the aching heart of Rosamond;

until at length she faintly replied, — "I may not go forth with thee, holy father, I must bear the bitterness of Eleanor's hatred, as a penance for loving Henry. Thou at least," added she, sinking down and seizing his hand, which she pressed to her beautiful lips: "Thou wilt know that when the grave has closed over the remains of the ill-starred Rosamond, she was not what the world will in after-ages believe her to be; that she sank quietly into the grave, bearing all the odium of her enemies, for the weal of the man she loved; that she preferred the peace of mind of her true lord, and the tranquillity of her country, to her own fair fame; that she was the wife of Henry of England, and not——" Her voice faltered, and her deep sobs sounded through the very heart of Becket, while her tears gushed forth like a summer shower.

"Weep not, fair daughter," said the Archbishop, assisting her to rise, while a silent tear stole down his own noble face. "This must not be, one word from my lips can make thee England's Queen; the Pope shall absolve me of the rash vow I have sworn to King Henry to keep his marriage with thee a secret. His Holiness will readily knock off this false fetter from my conscience. Fly with me to Rome, and thy claims shall be established before the eyes of a whole world; thou shalt no longer abide in this worse than dungeon. I have power, child, to drive the dark-hearted Eleanor from these realms, to send her back to the dotard Louis, who divorced her, or among the Infidels, with whom she carried on her unholy intrigues, even while dwelling in the camp of the soldiers of Christ. Let us haste, my daughter, and thou shalt speedily see that the Primate of England, the humble head of God's

Church in these realms, will seat thee in thine own high place, even although he may lose his own life in doing so just a deed."

For a moment pride and honour struggled in the bosom of Rosamond; and had they gained the mastery, Eleanor would have tottered upon her throne; and the territories of Poictou and Aquitaine vanished from Henry's grasp like a dream of the night, and peradventure war would have swept through the land like a dreadful hurricane; for Becket was not the man to resign the helm which he had once taken in hand, although he had awoke a tempest over his head. But love came to her aid,—love subdued by suffering, but flowing not the less deeply in her bosom,—a love that preferred Henry's peace to her own honour and ambition.—Even when her heart bled at every fibre, still she was the resigned,—the loving

Rosamond; and the anguish which at that moment wrung her heart,—could it but have been revealed—would have made the angels weep.

" No! no!" said she, conquering those deep emotions which shook her very frame; " this must not be; urge me no further on this matter. I believe thou meanest well to me and mine: but oh! consider what would be the consequence of this rash act.—I am unhappy now: I should be more so were this thing to come to pass. But even amid all my misery, I have still Henry's love. The bustle of a kingdom would but ill accord with me. I am not ambitious: I covet but peace, and with that, Henry; and while I have these, I can live happily in the meanest hut that shelters the serf. I am happy; and should covet nothing, could I but——" Just then the voice of her youngest child, which was sleeping on a couch

and covered with her mantle, arrested her ear,
and she flew as if to still its cries; but while
she bent over it, gave vent to a torrent of tears,
which her greatest effort could no longer withhold.

Becket turned away to conceal his own
feelings; and he who had withstood the King
in his anger, and confronted the whole array of
his nobles, without once allowing his feelings to
overcome him, stepped aside and wept like a
child, forgetting for the time his high station,
and all those dangers which dogged his every
footstep. Such is human nature in sensitive
bosoms; and the man who will not let a murmur escape his lips at his own sufferings, will
weep and sympathize at the sorrows of others—
albeit they are not so keen as his own—will
share the grief of another, when he would
sooner die than reveal the contending passions

which, like vultures, are tearing to atoms his
own heart.

"And this," said he to himself, "is the love
of woman.   Here then do I find an example of
fortitude that might become a god.   And am I
undergoing privation and suffering with such
disinterested motives ?   Does the love of God's
church alone impel me forward in this struggle,
free from pride and all ambition ?   Alas ! my
heart echoes not to these interrogations ; pride,
revenge,—a thousand contending emotions fly
up and repel its utterance.   But I will tear
them from my breast, although I drag flesh
and blood asunder with them."   He turned to
where the lovely mother was bending over her
child, and dashing the tears from his eyes, thus
ran his meditations :—

"What have I won for all the sacrifices I
have offered up on the altar of ambition ?

Would not a being like this have been a greater reward than all I have hitherto gained? But, alas! I must never utter the name of wife; never look into eyes that would resemble hers, and call me father. O God!" he internally prayed, " remove all these weaknesses from the heart of thy unworthy servant; make me fit to fight thy battles; give me strength to bear the armour which I have buckled on in thy cause; steel me against these human sympathies, which become not one who is wedded to heaven. 'Tis in vain," continued he, still pursuing the thoughts which emanated from his better nature, and sprang up in spite of himself. " Woman! thou art alone worthy to serve Heaven. She who would give up her own fair fame, — who would even sacrifice the honourable name of her children for peace and love, and the holy vow which she has made—

has taught a lesson to the high head of England's Church. Conscious that she will be
held innocent in the eyes of Heaven, she de-
spises the opinions of this world. Surely this
is pure,—this is devoted love! Henry of England, I will not serve thee worse than a woman.
I will keep faith with thee on this matter; even
if in the assembly of mine enemies, thine own
dagger was at my throat, I would die honest
to myself."

So ran the thoughts of the Archbishop of
Canterbury, while he stood gazing on the lovely
sufferer before him; and whether or not they
accorded with justice, it comes not within our
compass to say; they were, however, honourable to the man. And to such a pitch were
these scruples carried in that romantic and
even dignified age, that a man professing the
true principles of chivalry, was safe from the

most deadly enemy, who had once sworn to be secret and faithful in any matter. Becket, be it remembered, was a soldier before he became a Prelate; and although in the case of the articles of Clarendon, he did not in every sense adhere to his word; yet that was a matter that concerned the welfare of the church in a greater measure than his own private feelings; but in the present case, this was a vow sworn in friendship; and such a one as none but a craven or a villain could ever break. Nor was he one of those to be easily blinded by the power of Rome: for although he well knew that the Pope would readily absolve him from such a promise; yet he was aware that the motives which would lead him to seek the release, could only spring from a feeling of revenge, and add one more thorn to the eternal torturer, conscience.

It will, however, avail nothing to keep the curtain drawn over his inmost feelings. To say that he had never meditated seeking absolution from his vow, would be at once to write him down more than human, and to commit an outrage upon nature. Many a man is noble enough to forgive; but he who can bear persecution heaped continually upon his head, and having the power, meditates no retaliation, is in very deed a god. Men also in that age were influenced by the same passions which agitate us now. And although much of that ill feeling which at present rankles and frets in private, found vent in blood and sturdy blows; yet as in the present day, there were boundaries which could only be overleaped by a sacrifice of honour, and all that rendered the character of man valuable. And when Becket was persecuted almost to madness by Henry, when he remembered all he had undergone, and knew that even his life was aimed at, and if not sanctioned by the King, at least followed up by those whom he countenanced; no marvel if the thought flashed through his mind, and he was more than once determined to push revenge to the very verge of power.

After a long pause, Rosamond again approached the Primate, and on her knees implored his blessing before he departed. Becket placed his hands upon her beautiful head; and while his eyes were upturned towards Heaven, tear after tear stole silently down his cheeks; and although he spoke not, yet his lips moved as if in deep and fervent prayer. He then advanced to the door, and waved his hand in adieu; but twice did he return, as if he had yet something to impart to her, until at last he imprinted a kiss on her pale and cold forehead, and hurried out of the apartment, leaving Rosamond with closed eyes and folded hands, still kneeling on the floor.

The Archbishop hastened through the labyrinth, and followed by Gryme, rode on in the darkness until they reached the banks of the Thames, where a small boat was in readiness, when, having resigned their steeds to an attendant, they instantly embarked.

They pursued their course along the majestic river, sometimes mooring their little bark among the thick sedge when they were apprehensive of danger; then again dashing boldly along in the broad daylight, when their path seemed secure.

As they passed Westminster,—then bearing its ancient name, " The Isle of Thorns"—Becket gazed upon the hall of Rufus and the splendid Abbey, which had received many additions since the days of the Confessor, and thought that where then the jagged underwood and hoary hawthorns skirted the water-edge, while the minster and hall rose above, as if they had sprung up from the forest—that the day would come when goodly edifices should crown those banks, so dark with sedge and entangling thickets.

The boat shot safely through the narrow and pointed arches of the bridge,—which had then but recently been erected by Peter of Colechurch—and as the eye of the Prelate rested upon the Tower, which reared its old Roman remains, as if in triumph, above the Norman innovations, and pigmy turrets of the Bastard, he could not avoid recalling the mighty changes which the hand of time had wrought, and then reverting to those which he himself had undergone. They passed the steep acclivity of

Greenwich—then a wild forest which stretched for miles beyond what is now called Shooter's Hill, covering the broken ridges of Blackheath, and sloping down to the green vales of Eltham, and where now the old pensioners sit gazing over the lovely river, talking over their " hairbreadth 'scapes," herds of wild deer were congregated,—some browsing on the low and dense underwood; or bowing their antleredheads as they drank of the clear waters.—But what boots it following their course.—They gained the open channel, and their little bark rode safely over the ocean; although the darkness of November closed over their watery pathway, and the dying Autumn tore past with all its agony of storms.

They landed safely at Gravelines; and without halting, Becket, followed by the faithful monk, journeyed on foot to the monastery of St. Bertin's, near Namur; where we must for the present leave them, to attend to other matters connected with our story.

END OF VOL. II.

STEWART AND MURRAY, PRINTERS, OLD BAILEY.

CPSIA information can be obtained
at www.ICGtesting.com
Printed in the USA
BVHW041424120820
586210BV00003B/217

9 781379 262244